2/00 β

D1015163

CONSUMER TERRORISM

CONSUMER TERRORISM

How to Get Satisfaction
When You're Being Ripped Off

FRANK BRUNI AND ELINOR BURKETT

HarperPerennial
A Division of HarperCollins*Publishers*

Authors' Note

The information in this book is distributed on an "As Is" basis, without warranty. Neither the authors nor HarperCollins Publishers shall have any liability to the customer or any other person or entity with respect to any liability, loss, or damage caused or alleged to be caused directly or indirectly by the use of the advice contained herein, and any such liability is expressly disclaimed. Neither the authors nor the publisher are rendering legal advice, and the reader should seek the services of a qualified professional if legal advice is necessary.

CONSUMER TERRORISM. Copyright © 1997 by Frank Bruni and Elinor Burkett. All rights reserved. Printed in the United States of America. No part of this book may be used or reproduced in any manner whatsoever without written permission except in the case of brief quotations embodied in critical articles and reviews. For information address HarperCollins Publishers, Inc., 10 East 53rd Street, New York, NY 10022.

HarperCollins books may be purchased for educational, business, or sales promotional use. For information please write: Special Markets Department, HarperCollins Publishers, Inc., 10 East 53rd Street, New York, NY 10022.

FIRST EDITION

Designed by Joseph Rutt

Library of Congress Cataloging-in-Publication Data
Bruni, Frank.
Consumer Terrorism : how to get satisfaction when you're being ripped off
/ Frank Bruni and Elinor Burkett.
1st Perennial ed.
p.   cm.
ISBN 0-06-095196-6
1. Consumer complaints—United States—Handbooks, manuals, etc.
2. Consumer protection—United States—Handbooks, manuals, etc.
I. Burkett, Elinor. II. Title.
HC110.C63B78   1997
381.3'2—dc20   96-35390

97 98 99 00 01 ❖/RRD 10 9 8 7 6 5 4 3 2

Contents

CONSUMER TERRORISM

Introduction

A Call to Arms

When you calmly consider it, what did the American colonists really have to complain about? Sure, their tea was heavily taxed, but at least the salesperson undoubtedly smiled and gave them a good weight when they bought it each morning. These days, you're lucky if the clerk at the coffeehouse isn't gossiping on the phone with a friend, and if she merely overcharges you for your cappuccino by one dollar, it's probably the most accurate arithmetic she's done in months.

And what was the Unabomber all worked up about? Living in a low-maintenance cabin in the woods and getting around on a bicycle, he never had to deal with surly home repairmen who arrived late, if at all, and he certainly avoided auto mechanics who turned malfunctioning turn signals into engine overhauls that cost $1,500.

We know a real cause for revolution when we see one, and it's hardly taxation without representation or the unchartable frontiers of technology. It's the botched dye job for which you pay $100, the distracted waiter who brings you a martini when you asked for a margarita, the airline that loses your luggage, or the delivery that comes four hours late. It's a country in which goods have become so shoddy and service so sloppy that we are all too accustomed to expecting nothing more and all too ready to settle for even less.

The only sane response is a full-scale rebellion. We are here to sound that battle cry.

Think carefully: How many times have you stood across a rental car counter from a twentysomething clerk who behaved as if he were doing you a favor by taking your money and waxed irritated if you requested anything more elaborate than the keys to your car?

How many times have you gone out to get a scoop of ice cream, found that the assistant manager of the store had decided to lock up twenty minutes before closing time, and watched him refuse to even glance your way as you knocked on the door and flailed your arms in anger?

How many times have you boarded an airplane, watched it pull away from the gate, and then sat on the runway for two hours?

How many times have you returned a defective product or piece of clothing and been made to feel as if you had done something wrong?

Now: Imagine a country in which shopping for a new dress is actually a pleasant experience, shopping for dinner is actually an exercise in civility, the purchase of an appliance is not suffused with dread, and the wait for the elusive cable TV man is not awash in humiliation.

At this nadir in American consumerism, that utopia may seem exotic in the extreme. But if every American read this book and paid heed to its suggestions for just one month, that brave new world could be ours.

After all, what's standing in our way? Don't be a victim and blame corporate America. Those profitmongers will spend as little money as they can get away with, and we've been letting them get away with it for all too long. As a nation, Americans will brook no insult from even a second-rate dictator in Central

America or the Middle East. But as individuals, we're too polite to tell a workman that he's incompetent, too embarrassed at the thought that others might find us petty to argue over being charged four dollars more than the advertised price, too tired from the daily barrage of third-rate service and fourth-rate goods to demand our just due. We are, in a phrase, consumer sheep, letting corporate America lead us to slaughter.

Consumer Terrorism is a challenge to America—to all of America—to become tigers. We need to band together and declare our independence from bad service, haughty servers, voice-mail jail, and the hundreds of other petty annoyances that have converted the details of everyday life into a new circle in Dante's *Inferno*. The time has come to stand up, take up arms against the oppressors, and declare in one voice: "I'm tired of this shit and I'm not going to take it anymore."

This book is your guide through basic training, your road map to getting mad, getting smart, and getting even with the inept, aloof, and sometimes just plain larcenous merchants who dot this nation's strip malls and main streets, its inner-city corners and exurban intersections. Armed only with your ire, your voice, and the power of your wallet, you can storm the stores of this vast land and say, "Stick 'em up, buster, and don't ever mess with me again. (And say, shouldn't I get a rebate for my frustration, or at least a free side order of fries?)"

And it is fun. At its best, *Consumer Terrorism* brings an edge of agitation to an otherwise humdrum complaint. It gives you license to make someone else pay for every piece of garbage ever passed off to you as quality merchandise, every waiter who ever ignored your request, every salesperson who ever treated you like scum. It gives you back your power. It gives us all back our power.

This, then, is no run-of-the-mill consumer advocacy tract. We are not dispensing run-of-the-mill consumer advice. We've all heard plenty of that pap before, and what has it really gotten us? Perhaps, on occasion, a full refund on a patently faulty ware. But are we offered financial compensation for our trouble? Baubles for our pain? Do we emerge from consumer conflict in stores, restaurants, and hotels with the exhilarating sense that we have not only righted wrongs but actually triumphed? Have we inflicted a little pain of our own, sown as much misery as we reaped, struck a blow for downtrodden consumers everywhere?

Even Americans under the age of ten have at least heard about those seemingly apocryphal days when salespeople were friendly and honest, craftspeople took pride in their work, and manufacturers actually aspired to integrity.

What happened? During World War II, the nation discovered its own prodigious powers of production. Unfortunately, at the same time businesses and investors discovered that that same productive capacity could be turned into a gold mine. Small manufacturing companies run by owners for whom a good name was a point of honor were swallowed up or forced out of business by faceless conglomerates. Mom-and-pop stores where service was friendly and the produce always fresh couldn't compete with the bulk buying power of supermarket chains. A dizzying array of new consumer products gave rise to entirely new types of stores—almost all bastions of invisible buying.

After years of consumer deprivation during the Depression and the war, the American people were so caught up in the buying frenzy—in the excitement of new models of cars, the introduction of frozen foods, the invention of television and hi-fis—that we woke up only slowly to the reality that we were no longer doing business with friends and neighbors whose larceny was kept in check by social pressure, if not morality. Suddenly, we realized that we were hostage to anonymous corporations indifferent to quality, unconcerned about loyalty, and preoccupied with only the bottom line. After all, with both prosperity and the population boom, so many new customers were pouring through the doors of businesses that owners could afford to be blasé about satisfying old ones.

In that sellers' market, supermarket managers were all too willing to tell housewives to take their business elsewhere if they didn't like graying meat. If the furniture was too rickety for middle-class neighborhoods, manufacturers simply shipped it to the ghettos, where customers had few choices and new immigrants were coming in from the rural South.

Then, to make matters worse, business began to get "scientific," and its first experiments were on its own employees, who were boxed into rigid systems that controlled their every action and interaction. At the very moment that consumers most needed human beings to resolve their mounting problems, businesses were trying to transform employees from thinking, compassionate human beings into automatons who would spout corporate policy by rote.

The 1980s—that decade of business free-for-all—only made matters worse as Wall Street's demands for quick profits to stave off corporate takeovers turned the get-rich-quick mentality into a get-richer-quicker one. The raiders who counted weren't Ralph Nader's, and the federal government was too busy proclaiming our national superiority to do much about the sorry state of American quality and service beyond establishing an annual national quality award given out by some bureaucrats who've never asked us who deserved it.

By then—except for a few pockets where absurd prices brought superior service—the fine, subtle, and sensitive art of customer relations had dimmed into a fantasy. If Americans were stuck with shirts that unraveled after two washings or cars that were an exercise in planned obsolescence, so what? As long as businesses stuck together to rip off the American consumer, what choice would we have?

The fly in the ointment was the Japanese. They were feeding off the American consumer so successfully that their competition was growing lean. U.S. government and industry leaders blamed trade barriers, unfair competition, and other conspiracies for Japan's economic success, but consumers knew the truth: The only wily conspiracy being practiced by our neighbors to the east was the production of superior products.

The last straw was provided by the employment crisis that erupted as America moved from a manufacturing-based economy to a service-based economy. The number of high-paying industrial jobs suddenly decreased. More and more people were pushed into low-paying service jobs—and began taking out their resentment on the customers they were forced to serve. At other periods in the nation's history, the new service workers might actually have been grateful for their regular paycheck. But Americans had discovered their own entitlement, so even semiliterate teenagers with no education, training, or experience thought they were better than the jobs they held. They weren't grateful for their paychecks. They were pissed off that those checks weren't higher, that the guy in the head office was making more in a month than they did in a year.

Is it any wonder, then, that a great percentage of the men and women staffing the counters, answering the phones, patrolling the aisles, and interacting with customers at this nation's stores, restaurants, and hotels are ill-suited to the task?

Their discomfort and disgruntlement is made clear by the daggers they shoot at any customer who dares to ask them for anything more demanding than the time.

"There are all these people out there who once upon a time would have worked in manufacturing, but now they're in service, and they simply shouldn't be," notes Glen Goldstein, a New York City public relations executive who has begun to rebel against this trend. Goldstein has even gone so far as to take the phone company to small-claims court to sue them for his lost time waiting for a repairman to show up. "These people don't like being in service, and they're no good at it. If you don't have a service personality—if you don't find it challenging to make customers feel satisfied—there's nothing in the world that can train you to be that way."

Consumers, meanwhile, have been so beaten down by diminishing expectations that they rarely bother to raise a hue and cry, giving businesses the false impression that patrons are satisfied. For example, although New Yorkers are among the most vocal complainers in the nation, the city subway system gets just one-third the complaints per passenger mile of any transit system in North America. "My conclusion is that people are happy to have survived the trip," John A. Goodman, president of the Technical Assistance Research Project, told the *New York Times*. "They don't care if the seats are dirty as long as they haven't been mugged."

In fact, according to the National Consumer Survey, 70 percent of consumers never complain about faulty products or bad service—and that number might well be too low. Barry Reid, of the Governor's Office of Consumer Affairs in Georgia, told the *New York Times* that a poll in the early 1980s showed that for every consumer who complained about a problem, between ten and twenty consumers with similar disappointments simply slinked away with their tails between their legs.

But the tide is beginning to turn. American consumers might not be calling company complaint lines, but they are sharing their disgruntlement with their friends in record numbers. Consultants are taking note. One such consultant, Christopher Hart, warns his clients that unhappy customers tell their stories to an average of eleven people, who tend to pass these tales along to others in an ever-widening tree of ill will. By contrast, he estimates, happy customers only broadcast their contentment to six acquaintances.

That consumer grousing is just the tip of the iceberg. The gurus of business research have concluded that Americans are fed up with the way they are treated by the companies that provide them with the food they eat, the cars they drive, and the services they need to survive. The 1994 American Customer Satisfaction Index gave business a barely passing grade for pleasing customers, and the scores for 1995 were even worse.

As a result, loyalty to stores and brands has vanished along with the friendly clerk and the helpful merchant. Americans now feel free to take their business elsewhere, and are doing so in phenomenal numbers. In 1994, according to the Consumer Index, one-quarter of adult consumers switched their primary grocery store. One of the major reasons these customers cited was service.

Corporate America has read the surveys and reports, and the bottom-line guys are worried. So even while they downsize their workforces, they shell out record sums of money—an estimated $3.5 billion in 1992—for advice on how to turn the situation around. This is, more or less, the wisdom they have purchased for that sum:

- Consumers are becoming increasingly demanding. UPS delivers their packages across the country overnight, so why should a furniture store take three weeks to deliver a couch? Some auto dealerships offer loaners while cars are being fixed, so why should customers with broken computers be left without equipment for a month?

- Americans have wised up to the truth that most products are pretty much the same, so competition is keener than ever. If you want an edge, try offering good service.

- Companies that offer good service have higher profits than companies that mistreat customers.

- If you keep customers on hold, don't call them back, or keep them waiting, they'll be unhappy. Unhappy customers tend to have no loyalty.

- Buying loyalty is a worthwhile investment. Appliance manufacturers have calculated that each individual's brand loyalty contributes $2,000 to a company's profit over a twenty-year period, according to John Tscholl, author of *Achieving Excellence Through Consumer Service*.

- If you keep your customers, you won't have to cut your workforce. Boosting customer loyalty by just 2 percent has the same effect on the bottom line as cutting costs by 10 percent, according to Frederick Reichheld of Bain & Co.

The signs are popping up coast to coast: Some businesses have begun to heed the warning. Northwest Airlines has a whole program called service recovery, which often boils down to the issuing of $50 and $100 vouchers for customers whose experiences on the airline turn nightmarish. The insurance company Empire of America buys lunch for customers forced to wait in line for more than five minutes. First Union National Bank of Charlotte, North Carolina, delivers a dozen roses to clients who experience bank errors. Prism pest control, which specializes in commercial properties, promises restaurants and hotels that it will pay for the meal or room of any patron who spots a roach; Prism also sends that person an apology letter.

The moral is clear: If you want to throw off the shackles of your consumer victimhood, whip the country's businesses into shape, and shift the balance of power back into the hands of the little guy, now is the time. Seize the moment by reading on. All the strategies and inspiration you need are right here, in the following stories, statistics, information, and helpful hints.

Every movement has its cradle. For the American Revolution, it was Boston. For free speech, Berkeley. For newfangled militias, Waco.

For *Consumer Terrorism*, it was Lafayette, Louisiana, where we took a five-day business trip several years ago.

On the first day, there was little hint of trouble as we ensconced ourselves in a room at the local Hilton. We couldn't find a menu for room service, but when we called the front desk, they pledged to deliver one promptly. We muttered warm thanks.

On the second day, we began to feel less thankful. Our beds went unmade. Our menu never appeared.

On the third day—exhausted from hours of the serious journalism we usually practice—our desire for a menu ceased to be theoretical. We were hungry. We wanted food from what we feared might be mythical room service. "We're out of menus," the front-desk clerk told us this time. "Call the dining room and ask someone to read it to you." The staff of the busy dining room was not amused by that suggestion. They refused to help.

On the fourth day, we missed a business meeting because a phone message to the hotel was never delivered. Our beds again went unmade.

On the fifth day, we declared war.

"Let me speak to the manager," we said firmly into the phone. The manager was not available. We left a message. There was no response. We pursued the manager, hunted her down.

We discussed the matter of the unmade bed. "It is your responsibility to alert housekeeping if the maid doesn't visit your room," the manager insisted.

We discussed the matter of the room service menu. "Mistakes sometimes happen."

We discussed the matter of the phone message. "Mistakes sometimes happen more than once."

Her apology was perfunctory. We refused to accept it until she accepted responsibility. At a stalemate, we asked to speak with her supervisor, who was similarly obtuse about the emptiness of an apology with no dollar sign attached to it.

Declaring our intention to pursue this case to the highest echelons of the Hilton hierarchy, we asked for the phone number of the regional headquarters and the precise spelling of her name. She was not so obtuse as to miss the implication.

"Okay," she said. "When you come to check out, you'll see that we've taken something off the bill."

We didn't really care what that "something" was. Demanding compensation is, for us, both a principled position and an exercise in the Pavlovian reconditioning of corporate America. But that something turned out to be a reduction of more than $600 on our bill. All we ended up owing was $250—for a single night's stay and our phone calls.

The hotel, however, was not our only battlefield during that trip. We were also forced to take up arms against two other enemies: American Airlines and Budget Rent A Car.

A hurricane was bearing down on Lafayette—Andrew, that is, not us—and local authorities were poised to close the airport in New Orleans. Since Frank was due to fly back to Detroit and Elinor to Miami, a change in plans seemed appropriate.

"You're trying to take advantage of a natural disaster," an airline official groused when Frank asked if we could both be rerouted to fly out of Shreveport, Louisiana, instead of waiting to learn New Orleans's fate. It was a simple enough change of plans for us, since Lafayette is almost equidistant between New Orleans and Shreveport. And we were naive enough to think that American might actually be grateful to have two fewer New Orleans passengers to worry about.

Instead, we got fifteen minutes of invective, during which we gave as good as we got.

"Okay, you've worn me down," the American attendant finally said, changing our reservations.

The American clerk was mean. The Budget agent was merely moronic.

When we asked her if we could drop our car off in Shreveport, she seemed puzzled. "There's a hurricane on the way, and New Orleans is being evacuated," we explained.

"They're only recommending that people evacuate," she said.

"That's because the Constitution doesn't really allow the government to force everyone to leave," we responded.

"Gee, I didn't know the Constitution had a section on hurricanes," she replied with genuine interest.

We called corporate headquarters, demanding a representative who could beat a catfish on an IQ test. We didn't find one, but we did get our way.

That's pretty typical for us: We often don't find one, but we always get our way.

As we left Lafayette, one of us turned to the other, reflecting on our adventures, and asked: "Have we crossed some line from civility to all-out belligerence?"

The other responded: "We've become consumer terrorists."

And so we had.

And so should everyone.

FOURTEEN SUBTLE, AND NOT SO SUBTLE, WAYS MERCHANTS RIP OFF UNWARY CONSUMERS

1. Credit card companies lead you to believe that they have a single rate for all cardholders, but if you call the phone number on the back of your card and ask for a lower rate, more often than not you will get one—often a reduction of as much as 50 percent.

2. If you are female, you pay as much as 25 percent more than a man to have your clothes cleaned. (In one study, New York dry cleaners charged 27 percent more to clean a woman's white shirt than a man's—and the same price discrimination holds with suits, sweaters, and jackets.)

3. Businesses willfully "neglect" to credit charge accounts for returned items or deposits.

4. Banks lure customers with "free" credit cards, then tack on high annual service fees in the second year to make up the difference.

5. Utility companies fail to credit accounts when telephone service or power is shut off for a few hours or days.

6. Pharmacies give customers generic medications, but charge for brand names.

7. Companies routinely provide 800 numbers for orders but not for complaints. They do not offer to pay your long-distance charges when you call with a complaint.

8. Businesses expect you to pay the postage to return merchandise that is defective.

9. Airlines entice travelers with advertisements for incredibly cheap flights without explaining how few seats are available at those prices—or how many days those cheap seats are not available.

10. Funeral directors lead the bereaved to believe that a casket and embalming are legal requirements. A casket is not necessary if you are planning cremation, and embalming is not required if you are planning immediate burial.

11. The prices that come up for items scanned at checkout registers are often higher than the prices advertised on the store shelf.

12. When you return merchandise to a store for a refund, clerks frequently neglect to include the sales tax you paid in the amount they reimburse you.

13. Car dealers routinely touch up the paint on new cars scratched in transit and still sell them as factory-fresh vehicles.

14. Stores never offer to reimburse you for your parking when you have been forced to return in order to exchange faulty merchandise. If asked, however, they often will.

THE C.A.T. TEST
(For answers, see page 133.)

The following is a Consumer Aptitude Test. Take it now. When you finish this book, take it again. If your score doesn't improve, write to HarperCollins and demand a refund.*

1. You and your spouse show up at Le Bernardin in Manhattan, one of the most expensive French restaurants in the country, for an 8:00 p.m. dinner reservation. By 8:35, you are still waiting at the bar. You:

    A. Scream, "A roach, a roach," and then, as the restaurant empties, claim the table of your preference.

    B. Stagger out of the restaurant with hunger pangs and head for the nearest McDonald's, reasoning that at least the fries there are French.

    C. Tell the maître d' that if the restaurant does not pick up your bar tab for the entirety of your wait, you will not only leave the restaurant and never come back, but you will also call the authors of every restaurant reference book nationwide and everyone you know who makes over $100,000 a year to tell them that the steak tartare left you bedridden for a week.

    D. Ask if they need some help in the kitchen and roll up your sleeves.

*This is a lesson in reading the fine print. Who do you think you're kidding? Actually, we're kidding. HarperCollins will not refund one red cent.

E. Work up a set of tears, tell the maître d' that you have come to Manhattan all the way from Bismarck, North Dakota, to celebrate the remission of your wife's cancer, and that she may faint if not fed within five minutes due to her deteriorated immune system.

2. You go to the skin doctor because your entire body is covered with a rash, your regular doctor is stumped, and you desperately want relief. You linger in the waiting room for two hours, at which point you:

A. Give up on Western medicine entirely and go on a crystal-buying binge.

B. Run out to the nearest newsstand to supplement the selection of *Redbook*s and *Ladies' Home Journal*s in the reception area. Then, when it comes time to pay the portion of the doctor's bill not covered by your insurance, deduct the cost of the magazines.

C. Begin coughing violently, and, in close proximity to the woman in the reception area who most resembles Martha Stewart, say, "Oh, fuck, I forgot my TB medication at home."

D. Disrobe, at least partially, and badger the receptionist very loudly about scratching your back.

E. Leave, get in a warm oatmeal bath, and begin working the Yellow Pages for another doctor.

3. You purchase twenty-three dollars worth of groceries, including a glass bottle of mineral water, at the local A & P. The checkout clerk squeezes everything into one plastic bag, and as you hoist it by the flimsy handles into your trunk,

it breaks, plummeting to the pavement and breaking the bottle. You:

A. Kick aside the bag, take your receipt into the store, and demand money back for your purchases, saying that you are not going to pick through broken glass for the items that can be salvaged and that you do not have time to do the shopping over.

B. Sheepishly return to the store, apologize for littering their parking lot, and ask them for a broom and a dustpan.

C. Swear off glass bottles and vow to purchase only plastic in the future.

D. Salvage the undamaged items in the bag, bring your receipt into the store, and demand replacement of the broken bottle of mineral water.

E. March back into the store, demand to know the name of the manufacturer of the plastic bag, and threaten to file suit against that manufacturer and A & P for the eye you almost lost to a flying shard of glass.

4. Your interest piqued by a newspaper advertisement for a Sony stereo system at a special price of $600, you head to Crazy Eddie's. When you get there, they inform you that they have run out of the special at that store, even though the ad appeared that same day, and they suggest that you opt for an $800 system that's "really a better deal." You:

A. Leave in a huff and call the Better Business Bureau.

B. Thank them for the good advice and purchase the $800 system.

C. Ask them where another branch of Crazy Eddie's is located and then, in a tentative voice, ask for directions.

D. Grill them about the number of special units they had and why the advertisement didn't specify limited quantities, summon the manager, and demand that he locate the special at another Crazy Eddie's and have it delivered to your house lest you report the store to the state attorney general's office for bait and switch.

E. Begin screaming at the top of your lungs that it's not just the prices at Crazy Eddie's that are insane, but the entire management of the chain.

5. You purchase a loden coat at Eddie Bauer for $225. In the first week of wearing it, a button falls off, which you sew back on. Two weeks later, the lining rips at the shoulder, which may or may not have something to do with the fifteen pounds you gained. A week after that, you notice a fading in the color, which may or may not have something to do with the fact that you washed it four times in hot water. You:

A. Decide that you wear your clothing too hard and swear to confine all future shopping to Kmart.

B. Call Eddie Bauer and tell them that the coat started to spontaneously disintegrate within hours of its departure from the shop and that you want a new one express mailed to you along with a gift certificate to compensate you for your humiliation at having resembled a homeless person every time you wore it in public.

C. Go to the supermarket, buy a package of green dye, attempt to restore the color to your coat, then demand money back from the dye manufacturer when the coat comes out mottled.

D.   Wrap the coat in a box, put a bow on it, and make it a Christmas present for your nephew, who is college-age and strives for a grunge look.

E.   Move to a warmer clime.

6.   You make reservations to fly on American Airlines from New York to Denver, departing at 4:45 P.M. and, after a change of planes in Dallas, arriving in Denver at 9:30 P.M. The reservation confirmation from your travel agent notes that a meal will be served on the first leg of the flight. On that voyage, you are served a drink, an apple, and a cookie. On the Dallas–Denver flight, the fare is a drink and a bag of pretzels. By the time you arrive in Denver, you are faint from hunger. You:

A.   Write a letter to the president of American Airlines thanking him for helping you with your diet.

B.   Make a note to carry a sandwich on all future flights.

C.   Find the passenger service representative in Denver, explain that you are suffering a severe blood sugar reaction as a result of the airline's negligence, and demand a voucher for an immediate late dinner at an airport restaurant.

D.   Check into your hotel, order an expensive room service meal, and send the bill to the president of American Airlines with a demand for reimbursement.

E.   Check into your hotel, order an inexpensive room service meal, and fax a letter to the office of the president of American Airlines protesting the absence of meal service on a flight advertised as offering food and requesting compensation for your inconvenience and their fraudulent advertising.

7. You arrive at O'Hare Airport in Chicago and ask a cabdriver to take you to the Art Institute. Although you don't know Chicago well, you realize that you are getting progressively closer to Peoria and suspect that the driver is jacking up your fare by following an extremely circuitous route. You:

A. Don't care. You're on an expense account.

B. Politely ask the driver if he is lost and, when he insists he is taking a shortcut, start looking through your purse for extra money.

C. Duly note the driver's name and license number and file a formal complaint with the local taxi and limousine commission after your arrival at the Institute.

D. Refuse to pay the full fare when you arrive at your destination.

E. Warn the driver that you are feeling sick to your stomach and ask him to pull over so you can throw up. Then find another cab.

8. You purchase a Westinghouse refrigerator from an upscale appliance store for $1,679 and pay for it with your Visa card. The appliance is delivered, as scheduled, three days later. When you plug it in, you realize that the vegetable crisper is missing. You call the store, which promises to send a crisper over the next day. No one shows up. You call back and again

are promised delivery the following day. No one shows up. You:

A.   Call Visa and put the charge in dispute, get some friends to help you load the refrigerator on your pickup truck and unload it on the sidewalk in front of the store, then drive to a discount store and buy the same refrigerator for $1,195.

B.   Call Visa, put the charge in dispute, then go to a Westinghouse service center to buy a new crisper and send the bill to the appliance store.

C.   Call Westinghouse to complain about the dealer.

D.   Go to the Westinghouse service center, buy a new crisper, and send the bill to the appliance store— along with a bill for the time you spent waiting for your delivery.

E.   Stop eating vegetables.

The following is a test of your knowledge of consumer rights and laws. The questions come in different formats.

1. On a trip to Key West, Florida, you purchase a snorkeling mask for thirty-five dollars. When you return home to Chicago, you notice a crack in the plastic that was obviously there at the time of purchase. The owner of the Key West store, reached by telephone, refuses to refund your money. So you call Citibank Visa, whose card you used to purchase the mask, and ask them to put the charge into dispute. They refuse. Which one of you has the law on your side?

    A. You do.

    B. Citibank does.

    C. Both of you.

    D. Neither of you.

2. You go to a Tupperware party and, exhilarated by your introduction into the wide world of food storage, shell out $134 for plastic containers. Afterward, you have second thoughts. How much time do you legally have to cancel your order and receive a full refund?

    A. None.

    B. Two weeks.

    C. Thirty days.

    D. Three days.

    E. As long as you want, so long as the order has yet to arrive.

3. TWA bumps you from a flight between Detroit and Los Angeles and reschedules you for a flight departing five hours later. TWA is legally required to:

    A. Rent you a hotel room for your wait and give you a meal voucher.

    B. Give you a pass to its first-class passengers' club and upgrade you to first class on the rescheduled flight.

    C. Give you a voucher for a free flight within the continental United States.

    D. Pay you $200.

    E. Pay you $400.

4. You go to a bar on a Friday night and notice that they are offering women a happy hour special of two-for-one daiquiris. Is this legal?

    A. Yes.

    B. No.

    C. It depends on the state.

5. True or false: If you purchase a can opener that ceases to work after two weeks, but that did not come with a written warranty, you have no legal right to demand its replacement.

6. After two years of living in an apartment, you move out, leaving the premises in what you and the landlord agree is pristine condition. The landlord writes you a check to refund your $1,500 deposit. The figure on that check should roughly be:

A. $1,500.

B. $1,650.

C. It depends on where the apartment was.

7. You order a dress from the Spiegel catalog and are not told how quickly it will arrive. How much time does Spiegel legally have to send you the dress?

A. Fourteen days.

B. Forever.

C. Thirty days.

D. As long as it takes, providing that the company notifies you of any delay and receives your consent.

8. You wake up on a Tuesday morning, get ready to go to work, and realize that you don't have your wallet. You immediately call Visa and American Express to cancel your credit cards, but forget to call your bank to cancel your ATM card. When you realize your mistake three days later, you stop by the bank and are told that $1,000 has already been withdrawn from your account. How much of this are you responsible for?

A. $50.

B. $500.

C. The full amount.

D. None of it.

1
Basic Training

A few years back, Joanna Peck, a freelance management consultant who lives in Michigan, found herself in Texas on business. Not knowing Houston at all, she had booked herself into the downtown Four Seasons. She learned only after checking in that the best clubs and restaurants lay outside the city limits, accessible only by car. So, on one of her first nights there, she asked the concierge to recommend a restaurant in the suburbs and to summon her a taxi. With alacrity, he did both, and Joanna settled into the clean, spacious, comfortable backseat of her coach for what she had been led to believe would be a speedy, easy ride.

Twenty minutes later, she was still riding.

Fifteen minutes after that, she had yet to arrive.

Finally, some forty-five minutes after she had left the hotel, Joanna finally emerged from the taxi, forty dollars poorer and maddeningly flustered by the driver's inability to speak English and answer her questions about the length of the trip. Joanna didn't need a cartographer to tell her that his route had not been direct; if sketched out, she felt certain, it would resemble a loop-de-loop, or perhaps a figure eight. Her suspicions were confirmed when the taxi she took back to the hotel cut the trip by fifteen minutes and fifteen dollars.

Joanna had been stiffed, and she immediately hatched a

scheme for compensation. Marching briskly to the front desk of the hotel and adopting a firm tone to counterbalance the softness of her blond, petite, twentysomething presence, Joanna told the clerk about her big adventure, throwing in the fact that the restaurant had been awful. Moreover, she informed him, "I expect to be reimbursed for my strife."

When the clerk balked, Joanna asked for a manager and repeated her complaint. This time, she raised the ante with a stream of provocative observations and questions designed to let the hotel staff know they were dealing with someone ready and willing to inflict them with an enormous corporate headache:

- In taking on the responsibility of choosing and summoning taxis for its guests, wasn't the hotel also conveying an implicit guarantee of the service?

- In fancying itself one of the finest institutions in the so-called hospitality business, wasn't the Four Seasons inviting guests to entrust their care to the hotel and promising them a road map to a good time? When a recommended destination turned out to be aggravation and heartburn, wasn't the hotel betraying that promise?

- As it was, the taxi driver had run at least four red lights by her count. What if there had been an accident and she was injured? Might not a jury of her peers decide that the hotel could be held accountable and, to some degree, financially culpable?

"That was stretching it," Joanna concedes, "and I thought it might not fly, but it was all in the pursuit of getting some money back."

Predictably, it worked, as these carefully honed stickups usually do. The manager with whom she was dealing decided that Joanna's satisfaction and the good name of the Four Seasons were worth something, and refunded her fifty-five dollars, the cost of *both* cab trips. "I think that's great," she says, "even though I know a lot of people probably think I'm a bitch."

Au contraire, Joanna. We think you're a valiant warrior, worthy of promotion to three-star general in our consumer army. Joanna's handling of the Four Seasons demonstrates many of the bedrock tenets and tactics of consumer terrorism, which begin with a legitimate slight, but proceed from there in a much bolder manner than conventional consumer griping. What advice would the namby-pamby consumer advocates who guide Americans in their griping have offered Joanna? Take a peek. Have a laugh.

- "Write a letter," Marie Fonda Lloyd tells the readers in the October 1995 issue of *Black Enterprise* magazine.

Come now, Marie, why stop there? Why not a sunny postcard? A thank-you note? Don't spare the pretty stationery!

Give us a break. A letter often comes in handy at some point in a protracted consumer dispute because it becomes a formal document of both the nature and progress of a complaint, but it should almost never be the initial response. It's slow. It's easier to ignore than an increasingly irate voice tying up a valuable telephone line or, even better, a tantrum in the making in the middle of a store. And a letter offers the complainer but a tiny fraction of the visceral pleasure of voice-to-voice combat or full-frontal confrontation.

Consumer terrorism provides complete satisfaction. It's fun, it's pushy, and it provides an exhilarating departure from all those girdle-like manners your mother laced you into as a child.

- "Be friendly and smile a lot" is the milky pearl of wisdom from Judi Dash, writing in *Family Circle* about her own mother's faultless strategies for consumer satisfaction.

Clearly, what the Dashes should really be doing is advising beauty pageant contestants and politicians. As far as we're concerned, if a consumer terrorist is showing teeth, they should either be firmly clenched in a menacing manner or the subject of the dispute at hand.

- "Ask yourself whether you're upset about this particular issue or whether you're really angry about something else" is the advice of Amy Miller, a clinical psychologist consulted by the authors of a 1996 article in *Good Housekeeping* on how to complain and get results.

In other words, Joanna could have taken a moment, stepped back from the hotel's front desk, burrowed deep into her soul, and discovered that she was really in the grip of abandonment issues, or perhaps an Electra complex, lingering from childhood.

Consumer terrorism demands that you unlearn everything your mother, Ann Landers, Miss Manners, and every major consumer advocate ever taught you. It strikes a blow for justice without ever ignoring the restorative powers of revenge. Consumer terrorism is not a New Testament experience: There is no forgiveness here. This is the Old Testament: An eye for an eye, and maybe a nose and an ear as well.

As far as we're concerned, the only consumer advisor we've ever read who understands the game is Richard Feinberg, head of the Department of Consumer Sciences and Retailing at Purdue University, who advises customers tired of waiting in ridiculously long lines to knock on the company vice president's door and tell him to get behind the counter. "It may sound radical," he noted in an April 1995 article in USA Today, "but that's exactly what consumers need to do to get the attention they deserve."

Distilling consumer terrorism into a few succinct instructions is difficult. Consumer terrorism at its finest is fluid, adapting itself quickly and spontaneously to the demands of any situation. It relies on a quick wit, an acid tongue, studiously flared nostrils, and ingenious threats expertly designed to home in on an opponent's vulnerabilities. Consumer terrorism is not an exact science but a performance art—agitprop theater with a curtain call of financial booty.

But there are a handful of virtually immutable laws that will be refined and embellished in future chapters.

1: **Never shrug and never surrender.** Well, "never" overstates the case slightly; we hardly advocate an epic struggle over every ten-cent stick of gum that, due to a production error, packs insufficient flavor. But when you have been legitimately disappointed by a product or service for which you have spent hard-earned dollars and in which you have invested your trust and time, you deserve reimbursement and compensation. Pursue it. Pursue it even if the effort seems slightly out of sync with the potential result, because consumer terrorism is about establishing a pattern of complaint and combat that will ultimately change the behavior of service providers. Think of it as obedience school for a whole nation of unruly dogs.

2: **Strike quickly and forcefully.** Be bold. Stand your ground with confidence and panache, because you can rest assured that the person to whom you are delivering your complaint is sizing you up. If you seem like someone who will give up and go away quickly, you will be offered little or nothing. If you implicitly—or explicitly—threaten to disrupt your opponent's day, devour his time, and broadcast your woe to an ever-broadening circle of onlookers and friends, you will be offered something of significance. Self-interest rules in human behavior, and the clearer you make it that your unmollified anger carries a high price tag, the quicker your opponent will be to mollify it.

3:   **Shoot for the stars.** Demand more than a simple apology, and set your sights on compensation of some kind. Joanna had it down perfectly in saying, "I expect to be reimbursed for my strife." She left no doubt that she wanted a material measure of the hotel's remorse, but didn't box herself in by stating a specific demand that might have alienated her opponent instantly or, on the other hand, fallen short of what her opponent might ultimately have been willing to offer. You should, however, be ready to state the price of your satisfaction if your opponent asks. It should be more than simple reimbursement, and it should be deduced logically and persuasively.

4:   **Don't suffer fools.** Don't waste time on underlings, because these minimum-wage wastrels have little investment in your satisfaction and no power to effect it in any case. Most consumer bibles decree that you should work your way methodically up the ladder of a business's management hierarchy, rung by rung. While it's sometimes worthwhile to take a second or two to see if the clerk standing right in front of you can solve your problem, that experiment should be short-lived and fleeting if it doesn't yield immediate satisfaction. Seek someone with authority right away. In fact, make the phrase "Can I speak to the owner/supervisor/manager?" your opening gambit. This can trigger immediate results, because the underling with whom you are dealing may know that those people hate to be bothered and may devise a way to placate you even from his position of limited power.

5: **Wow 'em with facts (or at least factoids).** Brandish phrases like fraud, bait and switch, and product liability.

6: **Act like a librarian: file, file, file.** Develop your own Dewey decimal system for receipts and credit card bills for anything and everything you purchase, because you never know when you'll need them—and you never know when a mere $2.25 item will wreak damage or cause a headache worth $100. Keep a very careful record of the insufficiency of the product or service, the steps you have taken to complain about this, the time you have spent doing so, and every unsatisfactory response you have gotten in the course of the complaint. This casts you as a formidable opponent, but, even more important, it raises the specter of *evidence*, perhaps to be offered to the news media or used in a court of law.

7: **Find your opponent's Achilles' heel and shoot a flaming arrow toward its center.** Is this a business that faces keen competition and survives on repeat business? Threaten to take yours elsewhere. Is this a business for which public reputation and word of mouth are crucially important? Threaten to besmirch it. Is this a business tightly regulated by certain agencies? Know what those agencies are and threaten to contact them. The bottom line: Appreciate your leverage, and exploit it. This will be explored more fully in a later chapter.

8: **Refrain from outright nastiness; indulge in downright naughtiness.** You're playing a game of sorts, so have some fun. Consumer terrorism is permission to throw off the shackles of good behavior for a foray into constructive obnoxiousness. Any guilt you feel can be banished with a couple of simple questions: How many times have you been taken to the cleaners by a disreputable merchant? How many times have you paid good money for a bad product? The answer to both questions is plenty, and that's all the permission you need to turn the tables.

9: **Don't bother with the Better Business Bureau.** The greatest fiction of mainstream consumer advice is that the BBB is your staunchest and most effective ally, and it's a piece of shaky advice that American consumers have bought hook, line, and sinker. According to a Roper poll, 40 percent of disgruntled consumers first lodge their complaints with the BBB.

The BBB, contrary to many people's impressions, is not a government agency. To access information about those complaints, many BBBs use moneymaking 900 numbers that cost consumers plenty. Moreover, according to an investigation by *Money* magazine in 1995, the information is suspect. The magazine found that the BBB of Detroit granted the Gardner White furniture chain in Michigan a satisfactory rating despite the fact that nineteen complaints against it had been lodged with the state attorney general's office between 1992 and 1994. In fact, other complaints had been lodged with the BBB itself.

Worse still, the BBB's information can be woefully incomplete. One of *Money*'s reporters had to mention thirteen home improvement firms, eight auto repair shops, and six furniture companies in the Los Angeles area before it hit one in each category on which the BBB had files.

*   *   *

If you have any doubt about the efficacy of our methods versus the tame and tepid alternatives offered by others, if victory still seems an iffy prospect, consider a few of our own war stories.

Frank Picks a Bone with a Pet Merchandiser

A few years back, Frank bought his puppy, Pook, a beef-basted rawhide bone for something like $3.50 at the local pet super-store. Pook licked it. Pook nibbled it. Pook rolled it around the dining room rug. And when Frank gazed down lovingly to participate in Pook's pleasure, he saw that the basting on the bone had become mottled red marks on the white border of the rug.

Common sense might have told Frank this could happen, but he decided that the packaging might also have told him this. When he checked it, he saw no such warning. He marched back to the superstore with his receipt, his tale, and his pique. They refunded his purchase, but said the manufacturer would have to deal with his rug.

So Frank called the manufacturer, where a vice president first tried to insist that mere soap and water should eliminate the problem. Frank had soaped; Frank had watered. And yet he was certain that in particular kinds of lighting, at particular hours of the day, he could still see a hint of orange in the white border. So he insisted that the company reimburse him the cost of renting a professional steam-cleaning machine. Frank quoted them the twenty-five-dollar price for such a rental from a nearby supermarket. Days later, he received a check for precisely that amount.

Elinor Conquers Brother

Elinor hadn't owned her top-of-the-line Brother fax machine/copier/scanner for even a year when it began printing smudgy black lines down the center of her letters. Her husband advised her to shake the toner cartridge. There was no improvement, so she went to the store and replaced it. When the lines continued to transmogrify every word into an icon of Op Art, she picked up the phone to call the customer hot line at Brother International.

That, in itself, was a considerable challenge, for Brother has managed to create a maze of voice-mail jail from which few callers can ever finagle parole. Finally, she contacted a real person who insisted that Elinor needed a new drum, which cost $150. Elinor countered that no one should need a new drum after making fewer than one hundred copies and receiving fewer than three dozen faxes. The real person was not impressed, and led Elinor through a complex routine involving the pushing of buttons and the entry of secret codes into her machine that would, she was told, reveal precisely the number of pages her Brother had spit out.

When the number 8,012 appeared on the screen, Elinor exploded, "That's impossible." The real person was not fazed. "Machines don't lie," she said flatly.

Elinor wasted no more time with her, called the headquarters of Brother International in New Jersey, and asked to speak with the executive in charge of irate customers. After venting her ire and frustration, she accused Brother of setting the machine on 7,750 rather than o. The executive in charge of irate customers was cool. "There's no need for accusations and recriminations," he said. "Give me your name and address and I'll have a drum sent to you by Federal Express."

Elinor was dumbfounded when it arrived, as scheduled, two days later, and with no charge. There are, after all, some good companies left in America.

Frank Demands Credit for His Christmas Inconvenience

In the hurried, harried final days before Christmas one recent year, Frank raced through the shops in a suburban mall to rustle up presents for the family. He had already spent about $400 in various stores when a cashier suddenly informed him that Visa would not approve a $64 charge. The electronic authorization machine had flashed a message that no further charges would be approved until Frank called the bank.

Frank was incensed. His credit limit was at least $2,000, and he knew he was nowhere near it; he had not used the card in weeks—maybe months. Even worse, when he tried to call the bank, he wended his way through voice-mail hell only to learn that the department he needed closed at 5:00 P.M. and wouldn't open again until 9:00 A.M.

This was outrageous, because it was now 8:00 P.M., the stores would be open until 10:00 P.M., and Frank had planned on—had *depended* on—using those two hours to get ready for Christmas. It was the only window of time he had budgeted for shopping. Thankfully, he also had an American Express card with him, and pressed it into immediate service. But what would he have done if Visa had been his only card?

He called the bank the next day and let the woman at the other end of the line have it, detailing the inconvenience the bank had caused. (He left out the part about his American Express card.) She first took the tack that Frank should be grateful: The purchase had been denied because an automatic safety mechanism had been tripped by the sudden burst of activity on a card that was more characteristically dormant. "Did the automatic mechanism take into account that it's Christmastime?" Frank asked. She confessed it did not. "Why doesn't the automatic mechanism instruct the merchant to check my identification as opposed to sending me away?" She confessed she wasn't sure. So Frank told her that he would be sending her his shredded card in the mail because there were plenty of other banks that sent him credit card applications every week.

"I'll waive the annual fee of eighteen dollars for next year," she stammered.

"Just eighteen dollars?" Frank asked. "That doesn't feel like a sincere apology. I'm taking out my scissors."

"What *would* feel like a sincere apology?" she asked.

"Uh, fifty dollars," Frank shot back, wishing he had had more time to come up with a suitable figure.

"Okay," she grudgingly agreed. "We'll waive your annual fee and you'll find a fifty-dollar credit on your next bill."

Frank should have asked for $100.

MERCHANT-SPEAK: A GLOSSARY OF TERMS

Taking a store clerk, waiter, contractor, or business owner at his word is like believing Richard Nixon when he said, "I am not a crook." In fact, merchants have an elaborate and evasive code language of their own in which no statement conforms to its apparent surface meaning. A translation is necessary, and we herewith provide one.

"There's no supervisor here": *I've been threatened with immediate dismissal if I let another obnoxious customer interrupt my boss while he's eating lunch.*

"I'll have to check into that and get back to you": *Go sit in the corner and be quiet.*

"That's not our policy": *What you are suggesting will cost us money, so forget it.*

"We've never had this kind of problem before": *Lady, the* Titanic *had more satisfied customers than we do.*

"This would be so much easier if you had your receipt": *Aha! Got you on a technicality!*

"If you'll only be patient, I'm sure we can work this out": *Don't let the door hit you in the ass on the way out.*

"You're being unreasonable": *Go sit in the corner and be quiet.*

"That's not our fault": *The spontaneous unraveling of your cashmere cardigan must have been divine intervention.*

"We care a lot about customer satisfaction": *I put on deodorant this morning, what more do you want?*

"Are you sure?": *Liar, liar, pants on fire.*

"It was a computer error": *Go sit in the corner and be quiet.*

===============================

2

From Consumer Pushover to Pushy Consumer

Frank's mom, Leslie, was raised to be a consumer dishrag. She grew up in the Midwest, where civility and decorum were maintained at any cost, and came of age when Ike was the national father figure. In her upper-middle-class Protestant family, cleanliness was not quite next to godliness. Politeness was squeezed right there in the middle.

So Leslie never imposed on anyone; she avoided public conflict. She worried in particular that any fuss over money might seem tacky or be misconstrued as an admission of poverty. If she ordered her steak well-done and it came soft and pink in the middle, she just ate around the edges, reassuring herself that so much red meat wasn't healthy anyway. If the hotel chambermaid forgot to make her bed, she took care of it herself, telling herself that tucking in a sheet wasn't really so much trouble. If the electric bill arrived and was twice its usual amount, she never considered the possibility that the utility company might have made a mistake. She just figured she and the rest of her family must have been leaving on the lights.

Leslie was trusting, docile, and kind. A real lady. Merchants spotted her a mile away, pulled out their damaged goods, and jacked up their prices.

Then came the eighties. Little by little, Leslie began to feel that merchants were wiping the floor with her as never before. Instead of smiles, clerks offered snarls. Products were defective, professionalism was rare, and honesty seemed to have gone into full retreat.

But Leslie still clung to the lessons of her youth, despite egregious behavior on the part of service providers. In 1991 she and her husband bought a new home in Scarsdale, New York. Her life became a nightmare of contractors and workmen as she spruced up bathrooms, spit-shined the basement, and gutted the kitchen. It was the hardwood floors, however, floors that showed forty years of stress and strain, that drove her into consumer hell.

Leslie hired a specialist to sand and stain the existing hardwood floors in the front hall, the back hall, the living room, and the dining room, and to lay and stain a new hardwood floor in the kitchen. He quoted her a price of $3,500, $2,200 of which she paid while the job was still in progress.

But the job, except for the kitchen floor, turned out to be a disaster. The stain was supposed to dry quickly, yet days after the workers departed, it was still so sticky that Leslie and her husband couldn't walk on it. They had to exit and enter their house by climbing through a bedroom window. When her husband left for work each morning in his suit and tie, he hoisted himself over the window ledge and waited for Leslie to pass him his briefcase when he was safely on the other side.

Leslie asked the floor man to send his workers back to try again. They did—with identically sticky results. The window climbing went on for more than a week while the floor man tried to convince Leslie that her wood must have some unique property. She had enough good sense to distrust that explanation and hire a different floor company, which quoted her a price of $2,600 to finish the job. They had no trouble applying a stain that dried perfectly within twenty-four hours.

Leslie never paid the initial floor company the $1,300 she still owed them, but she also never demanded a refund of the $2,200 she had given them. Which meant, in the end, that she had shelled out $4,800 for her floors—$1,300 more than it was supposed to cost in the first place.

Leslie was so wed to her sense of propriety that when Frank first brought consumer terrorism into the family, she was at least as aghast as Mrs. Hearst when she saw pretty Patti with a rifle, beret, and brand-new revolutionary name. Imagine, for example, the family dinner at a Chart House restaurant in Hilton Head, South Carolina, when the Bruni party of ten was kept waiting in the lounge long past the time of their appointed reservation. After thirty minutes Frank declared that he had had enough and rose from his chair. Leslie turned pale. She knew from Frank's expression and gait that he wasn't headed for the bathroom.

"Please," begged Leslie.

"Oh, God, no!" gasped his father.

Despite their distress, Frank returned with the spoils. He had not so gently reminded the restaurant's manager that this party of ten was poised to spend a great deal of money, provided they didn't boil in anger and disgust and bolt the establishment. The manager responded by seating them almost immediately, sending them a complimentary round of drinks and shrimp cocktails and then picking up the tab for their desserts.

Frank was not surprised. Chart House, after all, is a nation-wide chain that can easily afford such largesse. But it astounded his family members and, over time, encouraged them. Little by little, his mother began to listen as he harangued her with the questions all strangers to consumer agitation need to ask themselves:

- Do merchants, salesclerks, and workmen show you enough integrity, sensitivity, or even humanity to merit your politeness?

- Are you getting what you paid for?

- If bad service and low standards go unchallenged, how will matters ever improve?

- Wouldn't you rather think of yourself as a champ than a chump?

- Wouldn't it be fun to tell your family and friends how you stood up to someone and won?

- Couldn't you use a good, stiff shot of adrenaline?

Leslie knew the answers to these questions. She knew she'd never survive without taking some lessons in consumer self-defense. And, gradually, she began to change. At first, the change was barely noticeable — a refusal to smile at an errant clerk or a quick stride out of a store where customers are ignored.

Then one day she called the electrician and asked him to install a new chandelier over the kitchen table. When he opened the box, he could find only five glass globes. The chandelier was designed for six. Leslie snapped. Not even bothering to try to solve the problem by telephone, she freshened her lipstick, threw on her mink, and drove straight to the lighting store to demand the missing globe.

"That's a special order," the saleswoman responded. "It

could take weeks." Leslie rolled her eyes heavenward in frustration and was suddenly visited with an inspiration: There, hanging from the store ceiling, was a model of the chandelier she had purchased. Glittering along its brass-and-stainless-steel limbs were six globes.

"I'll take one of those," Leslie said, pointing to the fixture. "*You* wait for the replacement."

The saleswoman's jaw dropped, forcing the lower of her two chins to quiver. "You can't have any of those," she jabbered. "That's the model."

"Listen, I have an electrician waiting at my house *right now*," Leslie countered. "I'm not leaving without that globe."

The standoff began, and Leslie almost caved in to habit and discomfort as she stood eye-to-eye with the saleswoman. Only the thought of Frank's lessons emboldened her. She did not surrender. Finally, with a huff and more than one puff, the saleswoman fetched a ladder, hiked up her skirt, and, teetering in high heels, ascended the rungs to collect Leslie's due.

Leslie rushed home and called Frank. She was giddy. She had her globe. More important, she had a new lease on her consumer life, a sudden hope of transforming herself from victim to victor. She was not yet wielding a consumer Uzi, but she was at least packing a Swiss Army knife.

Leslie is living proof that even the unlikeliest recruit to consumer terrorism can take up arms if given the proper prodding and praise for each small step toward power. Don't say you can't do it: Forget the *Maine*, remember Leslie.

Like her, however, the fledgling, novice consumer terrorist should make his or her initial forays and opponents small and relatively unintimidating ones. Be gentle with yourself as you learn how to steel your nerves and assert yourself.

After her globe triumph, Leslie began checking her grocery

receipts and, when she found overcharges, started returning to the store to collect what was owed her—no matter how modest the amount. She started disputing inflated items on her hotel bills and had them successfully deleted. She even occasionally called a utility company with a pointed question about her bill.

Leslie learned to stand her ground, and, more important, she discovered that even when she thought she couldn't press for another minute, she could always find a way to push herself a little bit further. It's just like the first weeks at the gym: You're finding and flexing a new set of muscles, and they'll get bigger and stronger with repeated use—and repeated reward.

As Leslie began to rack up her successes, which were immediate and many, she began to find and fashion her own personal style and modus operandi. Some consumers feel most natural levying their complaints in a voice of barely controlled fury. Others, like Leslie, prefer prim determination. Never wanting to appear like someone spoiling for a fight, never wanting to bludgeon a merchant into submission with the threat of causing a scene or spreading poisonous word of mouth, she eschewed what for many is the viscerally pleasing rush of wallet-to-cash-register combat for the subtler art of ethical persuasion—a posture of heartbreak, disillusionment, and betrayal that works its own magic. In other words, she brandished the weapon of moral superiority—and the following tale illustrates how deadly accurate that implement can be.

In early 1996, as she drove home from a doctor's appointment, Leslie experienced a sudden craving for an avocado. The nearest place to buy a decent one was Hay Day, an ultra-gourmet grocery store where a concierge sits at a reception booth near the entrance and half a dozen bananas cost as much as a lamb roast might in an ordinary supermarket. So Leslie stopped at Hay Day, bought herself an avocado for $1.49, and went home with visions of an imminent feast of fat—avocado, cheese, and mayonnaise on toast—dancing in her head.

The ballet came to an abrupt halt when she cut into the avocado and found that it was rotten. In normal circumstances, Leslie might have done nothing more than throw it in the trash. But she had spent thousands of dollars at Hay Day, where the steep markups are supposed to ensure against inconvenience.

So she put the rotten avocado in a bag, took it back to Hay Day, and requested a refund of $1.49. It was slow in coming, as Leslie describes in the letter she subsequently sent the manager of the market. (Yes, it's true that she broke our cardinal rule about letters, but remember, the point is to develop your own style, and Leslie certainly has style.)

I was first told by your concierge that I didn't purchase the avocado at Hay Day, even though I had the register receipt, because you didn't carry that brand. When I asked to see the manager, I was left waiting for an inordinate amount of time while it seemed everyone was checking to see if I could have purchased the avocado at Hay Day. Whereas you eventually issued me the refund, I was left with the definite impression that all of you felt I was returning merchandise purchased elsewhere.

Possibly, in this day and age, you have a problem with dishonest customers. . . . It seems we now live in a world where everyone tries to "stick it to" everyone else. I am of a different generation and have always taken pride in honesty, fairness, and especially my reputation. To find my word being questioned is extremely offensive.

I have enjoyed shopping at Hay Day since your opening and have spent an extravagant amount of money on the terrific steaks and tenderloins my family loves. . . . I regret that I shall

probably never feel quite comfortable shopping . . . at Hay
Day in the future.

As a former retail buyer, I deplore the fact that customers
are treated with less respect than cattle in a majority of
retail establishments. It seems only Nordstrom affords the
consideration and courtesy customers deserve. I had thought
Hay Day did too. I am genuinely disappointed.

Leslie could have laid it on even thicker than that. She could have mentioned that the doctor's appointment from which she was returning when she bought the avocado was a session of chemotherapy and that she had been battling terminal cancer for nearly seven years. She could have mentioned how difficult it is for her to keep her weight up—how one lost meal is no small disruption. She could have because all of that is true. But she restrained herself, and probably helped her case, coming across as a beacon of sober, rational reflection.

Several days later, Leslie received a call of apology from the manager. And several days after that, when she returned home from an errand, she found a note on her doorstep from the manager. It offered yet another apology: "I hope we'll see you in the store soon and you'll afford us the opportunity to restore your faith in Hay Day." The note rested in a lovely basket brimming with flowers and a veritable orchard of avocados.

Not one of them was rotten.

THE TWELVE STEPS TO CONSUMER EMPOWERMENT

1: Admit that you have a problem: namely, a tendency to let merchants and businesses treat you the way Joan Crawford treated her children, and with similar impunity.

2: Turn for guidance to a higher power—namely, the authors of this book.

3: Jettison politeness and tact unless they are reciprocated. Miss Manners might not approve, but then Miss Manners probably never purchased a washing machine with a defective spin cycle.

4: Realize that merchants fear you as much as you fear them. They do not want to lose your business. Your best weapons are your ability to take it elsewhere, hold hostage their time, and impugn their reputations with negative word of mouth. Begin using all three.

5: Accept that you, the consumer, are always right—or almost always right. On those rare occasions when you are wrong, well, the target of your aggression will simply have to get over it.

6: Do not be afraid to demand satisfaction and suggest compensation for the hassle of having to make that demand. Wed anger to avarice. When necessary, bawl for dollars.

7: Tempting as it may be, do not threaten to sue. Merchants are well aware of the prohibitive cost of retaining a lawyer and the unlikelihood that a consumer will do so.

8: Eschew cathartic mischief-making or acts of vandalism. Revenge is sweet, but not if it gets you arrested.

9: Learn these words (let them become your consumer mantra): "I would like to talk with your supervisor."

10: Keep a list of all the ways in which companies have harmed you and, in weak moments, use it to bolster your resolve that it will never happen again.

11: Educate yourself on the various and sundry consumer laws at your disposal and wield them like a poison-dipped dagger.

12: Having had a spiritual awakening as a result of these steps, commit to sharing them with other consumer victims and practicing these principles for the rest of your consumer life.

3

Stockpiling Your Munitions

Leslie Bruni's letter to Hay Day featured several master strokes, including the portrait she painted of herself as a paragon of honesty and the reference she made to another store, Nordstrom, that put the one she was battling to shame. But neither of those elements was the decisive factor in her victory. Her trump cards were her twin assertions that she had spent gobs of money at Hay Day in the past and that she might not spend another cent there in the future. She thus created a powerful motive for the manager of Hay Day to make her happy. And that is precisely what the manager did.

Successful consumer terrorism always begins with a careful assessment and appraisal of how much power you hold in a given situation and how you can best wield it. Consumer terrorism is, then, in the beginning and the end, a matter of leverage, and while the amount of leverage you have is bound to vary widely from one situation to the next, you always have some. You simply have to divine what it is, define it, and figure out the precise window of opportunity for its use.

The most obvious portal is the one Leslie used: the threat of lost business. When employing this strategy, it is wise to amplify or even exaggerate your patronage of a business. A little melodrama never hurts.

Don't say: "I've bought many things at Sears over the years and never had this kind of trouble."

Say: "Sears has been at the center of my family's life for generations. I feel so betrayed, and I'm not sure I will ever get over it."

Don't say: "TGI Friday's is usually better than this."

Say: "I've never loved another restaurant's burgers or desserts the way I love the ones at TGI Friday's. I bet I've eaten more than one hundred dinners at Friday's around the country. But after what I've been through tonight, I guess I should consider this the last supper."

Don't say: "I was accustomed to a pleasant shopping experience at the Gap and am surprised by this treatment."

Say: "I can't think of a single clothing store in which I've spent more money than the Gap, and I'm the thoroughbred of clotheshorses. I guess I'll have to gallop down a different track."

Okay, so the last metaphor is a tad overboard. But you get our point, which is to make sure that the clerk or waiter or merchant with whom you're dealing gets yours.

You should know from the start that just as your leverage as a consumer varies, so does the receptiveness and vulnerability of the business you are patronizing. You can figure out your chances of success—and, thus, how and for how long you should press on in your consumer offensive—based on the following questions:

1. *How big is the business to which you are laying siege?*

Figuring out whether the business's size helps you or hurts you is a little like reading tea leaves. If it is tiny—say, a mom-and-pop store that operates only in a single location—you may be in trouble. A business like this runs on a skimpy profit margin, so it cannot afford to absorb significant losses just to ensure future business. Also, you rarely have the option of climbing the corporate ladder with your complaint in order to find a sympathetic ear. There is no corporate ladder.

But this is not a hard-and-fast rule. Many small businesses are keenly aware of the fact that they live or die in a sea of chain stores by the grace of customer loyalty. If that's the philosophy of your opponent, you have enormous power. Wield it cautiously, however, lest you make it so difficult for such businesses to survive that you and all other consumers are left only with monolithic, anonymous emporia.

If, however, the business is big—say, one outpost or franchise in an enormous chain—you are guaranteed two things: a multilevel hierarchy of people to complain to and the company's ability to absorb short-term losses for the sake of long-term loyalty.

2. *How unique is this business's services?*

If it has little competition, the balance of power tips in the store's favor. For example, if you live in a small town with one plumber, demanding that he trim some of the fat off his bill because the job took two weeks longer than he projected is a gambit with dubious prospects of success.

If dozens of local businesses duplicate the services of the one you're battling, however, you're sitting pretty. The executives at the Gap—to revisit that store as an example—know that the suburban turf on which most of their franchises sit also accommodates countless other shops with relatively similar wares in a relatively similar price structure. So they need to keep customers happy with the Gap if they want them to continue shopping there.

3. Is this the kind of product or service that you will be purchasing time and again in the future? Does the establishment rely on repeat business? Does it rely, as well, on good word of mouth?

If the answers to these questions are yes, then you and your complaints have enormous muscle, particularly if you know how to flex it. Most shoppers, for example, visit their favorite clothing store several times each year; the store should appreciate that, and if they don't, reminding them of it is a great way to get them to snap to attention.

Most restaurants live or die on recommendations from satisfied patrons and cannot afford to let too many walk out the door with grimaces on their faces. In any dispute, you should make it absolutely clear that you are a notorious blabbermouth, the kind of person who relishes sharing your horror stories with anyone who will stop to listen. Don't be afraid to recite your résumé, or even embellish it with a carefully chosen fib or two, to any merchant or executive who doubts your ability to spread the word far and wide.

Do you work in an office with hundreds of workers whose paths you cross at the water cooler? You might want to allude to it. Are you president of your block association or an officer in the local PTA? Wave that banner. Do you belong to the chic country club in town or have high-placed friends in government? Well, there's no shame in furnishing your enemy with a succinct autobiography.

* * *

Let's revisit Joanna Peck, whom you met on her adventures in Houston, because she is a master at the game of artful leverage. Perhaps this talent is genetically encoded in her: She began demonstrating it when she was only seventeen.

It was at that tender age when she waltzed into a Macy's in suburban Maryland with a teenage girl's fantasies of instant beauty and cosmetic glamour. She stopped at the Princess Marcella Borghese counter, where creams and potions and blushes in a dazzling array of colors winked at her from beneath pristine glass counters. She didn't have all that much spending money, but she decided to blow twenty-one dollars on a tube of lipstick that promised an all-day sheen without fading or smudging.

A few days later, she fished the lipstick out of her purse, slid off its top, and saw that it had disintegrated into cakey pellets. She was crestfallen. "I may have spent only twenty-one dollars," she recalls, "but to me, at that time, it was like one million dollars."

Joanna raced back to Macy's for a refund. The woman at the counter instead offered her an exchange. Even at seventeen, Joanna knew this was ridiculous: Why would she want another tube of a lipstick with such fickle properties? She asked for a department manager, who also refused to give her a refund. Then, operating on sheer instinct and her Italian-American family's zest for loud confrontation and conflict, she demanded to see a customer service representative.

She ended up in the office of the store's marketing manager, who adopted a parental, condescending tone of voice. Joanna was suddenly aware of her wardrobe—jeans and a sweatshirt—and the fact that she had not washed her hair that day. To this man, she realized, she must look like some scruffy little hooligan. How could she sway him? Thinking quickly, she said, "I don't have a charge card here. But my mother does. And if this isn't resolved, my mother will never shop in this store again and neither will my father."

To which the manager uttered an astonishing "That's okay with me."

Joanna called his bluff. She had her mother phone the store's general manager. "How could Macy's treat my daughter this way?" her mother asked, appealing to what she hoped would be his sense of pride in his store. Then she appealed to his heart and to his business logic: "Maybe my daughter is just seventeen and isn't your biggest customer, but someday she might be. In any case, I don't know how you could make her so unhappy on this day, when we're having her high school graduation party." Then the final kick: "I'm going to give her twenty-one dollars from my own purse so she can go to another store and buy a tube of lipstick."

It was brilliant. Macy's sent Joanna and her mother not only a twenty-one-dollar check but gift certificates that totaled about sixty dollars in value. Plus, the manager offered to buy Joanna and her mother lunch in the Macy's restaurant the next time they came into the store.

Joanna had intuitively understood that she had leverage above and beyond her own threats, and Joanna's mother cannily comprehended the various ways in which her appeal could register most forcefully. Joanna has since graduated to ever greater summits of consumer aggression and victory. A psychological and tactical appraisal of her opponent is always the key to her success, she says.

Here are a few pieces of advice from Joanna: If you are dealing with some lunk who clearly feels that giving you what you want is a surrender of his masculinity, move on immediately to his superior. If you are dealing with a store that's been a bedrock in a given community, appeal to the establishment's sense of civic pride. If you are dealing with a store that's being threatened by an up-and-coming competitor, mention your better experience with that new business or your curiosity about it. If you are being dismissed because you are too young or too old, ask the person dismissing you if he or she would want his or her child or grandparent treated this way.

Case in point: While living briefly in Manhattan, Joanna had a dispute with her landlord. (If you've ever lived in Manhattan, the aforementioned fact is a statement of the obvious.) The heat was intermittent and a rat actually ran across her bed one night while she was in it. So she withheld two months of rent—a total of $1,200—until the landlord fixed the heating system and adequately exterminated. Only then did she start paying rent again. Even then she did not pay the $1,200.

Her landlord kept demanding that money, even threatening to take her to court, so she realized it was time to devise an approach other than a flat "No." Surveying her options, she seized on the fact that her landlord was a Hasidic Jew who was typically protective both of women and of his own teenage children, who happened to be close to Joanna's age. "How would you feel if your daughter were living in a place where a rat actually ran onto her bed?" she asked one evening. "Would you feel she owed her landlord any rent?" It worked. The landlord forgave her debt.

While emotions can sometimes work wonders, information is a more reliable ally. Knowing everything you can possibly know about a business or company and the industry in which it operates gives you extraordinary leverage—and that information is easily available in a world of public information. Hotels, for example, depend on and care deeply about the esteem in which they are held by guidebooks and travel agents. That means that in an unresolved spat, you should make it clear that you are willing to spread news of your gripe in these directions.

The makers of appliances or building materials have certain large chain stores—Home Depot and Builders Square, for example—that buy an enormous percentage of their wares. That means you can threaten to make your dissatisfaction, and their sins, known to the merchants they supply, and thus give those merchants pause about an alliance with a company that leaves angry consumers in its wake.

Many trades have associations or trade publications that, at least to some degree, monitor them; knowing the names of these groups or periodicals, and brandishing that knowledge at a key juncture in a standoff, can be extremely useful. The agenda here isn't to actually lodge your complaints in these other venues, because consumer terrorism is not meant to be time-consuming. The goal is to wield as many threats as possible, to load your quiver with a wide array of arrows. If nothing else, your opponent will register your seriousness and resourcefulness. That alone may be all the suasion you need.

If a company is publicly traded, that means they have stockholders who, theoretically at least, care about that company's performance, if not behavior. And a list of those stockholders is only as far away as your own home personal computer, providing you have a modem and Internet access. All you have to do is log on to the Security and Exchange Commission's site and download all the major stockholders and officers of a given company. Even if you are computer illiterate, you can still tell your opponent that you are aware of this power and willing to exploit it. And if your complaint involves enough money or fills you with enough passion, go ahead and start a mailing campaign. The bigger the headache you threaten or create, the greater the motivation a business has to make you go away.

Even businesses that would seem immune to your dissatisfaction have points of vulnerability. Utilities are a prime example. Most telephone, electricity, gas, water, and cable television providers have monopolies on their markets, but states have set up regulatory agencies and public service commissions so that irate customers who cannot simply take their business elsewhere have some way to seek amends and apologies.

New York State, for example, has a Department of Public Services that logs complaints from utility customers and sometimes steps in to resolve disputes. Moreover, the state reserves and exercises the right to deny utility companies rate increases or penalize them if they have maintained poor consumer satisfaction records. Something else you should know: Many public utility commissions have a rule that once you have formally registered a dispute with the utility, you do not have to pay the charge under dispute until the situation has been resolved. (You should, however, pay the rest of your bill.)

In all kinds of situations, you can invoke the fact that the local newspaper or TV station has a consumer complaint line: The prospect of your scuffle reaching hundreds of thousands of readers or viewers should make many a merchant budge. You can demonstrate your familiarity with the fact that the attorney general's office in every state has a consumer fraud division. You can allude to your familiarity with the civil rights protections of your given state or municipality if there is any hint that the way you're being treated smacks of bigotry.

That last gambit is a bit of leverage that our friend Robin Haueter failed to grasp when a washer and dryer he purchased became the agents of considerable dismay. He bought the appliances not at a discount store, where service is notoriously horrendous, but at a sophisticated establishment whose stock of high-end European brands assured him he was in genteel hands. The salesman was courteous. The transaction— $1,081.36 for a Whirlpool stacking washer and dryer with stand—took fewer than ten minutes. Delivery was promised within four days. Robin walked away with a smile on his face.

It didn't last long. The appliances arrived without the stand, which the salesman blithely informed him was out of stock. "We'll call you when it arrives—two, three days tops," he said. There was no remorse, and no apology.

Robin never found out whether the salesman would have called. The next day, when he turned on the dryer, the stench of burning wires filled his apartment and the calm whir was quickly drowned out by a clangorous banging. When Robin called the store, he was turned over to Max, who directed him to call Whirlpool. "They'll send someone over to see if they can fix the machine in your house," Max said. "If they can't, then they'll authorize its return."

Robin didn't want a repairman to fix the dryer on his newly refinished maple floors. He wanted a new machine. He spent three days on the phone with Whirlpool—often on hold listening to recorded tips about ingenious uses for ice cube trays—trying to plead his case with young, innocent customer service representatives.

Not entirely naive, he did ask to speak to a supervisor. "He's out to lunch," the Whirlpool representative responded without clarifying whether the comment was literal or figurative. "Try the president," she suggested. Robin did not heed her advice.

Ultimately, he was told in brusque—and no uncertain— terms that the problem was the store's, not Whirlpool's.

Robin called the store again, demanding to speak with someone in charge. That someone identified himself as Bobby and offered a surname that was the same as that of the establishment. Robin breathed a sigh of relief. "Finally, someone with authority," he thought as the man listened to his complaint, clucked over Robin's inconvenience, and vowed that the machine would be picked up and replaced and the dryer stand delivered within four days.

The new dryer arrived promptly, but no stand was included. Robin called Bobby again, but Bobby claimed not to remember who Robin was or what had happened up to that point. Robin repeated his tale. He was promised a phone call, and delivery of the dryer stand, within four more days.

A week later, still waiting, Robin called Bobby once more. And once more Bobby remembered neither Robin's name nor his problem. "I'm so sorry," he said after Robin reeled off his tale. "We'll get Whirlpool to deliver it to you directly."

By then, Robin was getting a tad testy. "That's nice," he said, "but when?" Bobby pledged that he would find out and call Robin back right away. This promise, like the others, was empty.

"Can I speak to Bobby?" Robin insisted when he rang the store yet again. By this point, he had memorized its number.

"Which one?" the receptionist asked. Robin mentioned the name of the store.

"There's no one here by that name," she replied, and suggested that he might be looking for a Bobby with an entirely different last name. Robin was shocked—and considerably less pleasant—when he heard Bobby's now familiar voice.

"Hold on, hold on, let me get someone to help you," Bobby said, passing the phone to Robin's old friend Max. Max didn't even try to be pleasant. He simply insisted that the stand had already been delivered. Only after Robin became insistent did he grudgingly agree to double-check the detail and call back.

Two days later, when Robin placed his sixth call of complaint, Max too seemed lost in a fog of willful forgetfulness. Robin, at last, began to lose his temper and, for the first time, raised his voice.

Just before Max summarily hung up on him, Robin heard him proclaim to someone else at the store: "You should hear this guy. Queer as a three-dollar bill."

Three more calls and one week later, the dryer stand finally arrived—in a box that was covered with bird shit and missing two essential pieces. And Robin, too busy to bother with this mess, gave up. Besides, he thought, what recourse did he really have?

In fact, he had excellent recourse above and beyond the usual methods. When Max uttered his comment about the three-dollar bill, he did so in the wrong geographical location: New York City, which, like a few dozen other progressive urban areas of the country, has legislation forbidding discrimination based on sexual orientation. Robin could have brought this to the store owner's attention and threatened to file a complaint with New York City's Civil Rights Commission. While the commission was unlikely to find that Robin's harassment fell within its purview, the potential hassle for the store might well have moved them toward some accommodation with their unhappy customer.

Moreover, Robin could have pointed out to them that he was a well-connected citizen of Manhattan's gay community, many members of which lived in the East Village neighborhood where the store gets its customers, and that he was willing to take his story public at any and all gay forums he could find. Even if the store proved as immune to this prospect as they did to every other aspect of Robin's complaint, they would surely have felt the sting of some lost business if Robin had proceeded with this tactic.

And today he would feel like the bully, not the bullied.

DOS AND DON'TS

While consumer terrorism is an aggressive enterprise, it is not an unscrupulous one. When in the right, you should take no prisoners. When in the wrong, you should not fire even a warning salvo. And you should never, ever resort to illegal strategies of war.

Here are some examples of acceptable and unacceptable complaining.

Unacceptable: A woman buys a dress that fits her perfectly, wears it to a special, one-of-a-kind event, and then, figuring that it's still in perfect shape and she will never don it again, restores the tags to the dress, boxes it up, and returns it to the store for a full refund. This is wrong, illegal, and antithetical to more consumer power. It engenders suspicion between customers and merchants, who estimate that they lose $1 billion a year to returns fraud, according to a June 1996 article in *USA Today*.

Acceptable: A woman buys a gown that needs altering, then returns not once, not twice, but three times as the store seamstress repeatedly fails to tailor the dress correctly. At this point, the woman demands a full refund, figuring that the material in the dress cannot have been unaffected by repeated alterings. The woman also demands 20 percent off the purchase of a replacement dress for her inconvenience and lost time in revisiting the store so frequently.

Unacceptable: When Peripheral Outlet, which sells Macintosh computer memory from a base of operations in Oklahoma, failed to make a promised overnight delivery to a customer in New Hampshire, the man sued for reimbursement of his shipping charge. What the man failed to take into account, or to forgive, was that New England had been hit by a terrible, transportation-crippling blizzard on the night in question.

Acceptable: Frank bought a desk from Staples, which agreed to deliver it on a Monday, sometime between 9:00 A.M. and 5:00 P.M. The Friday prior to the promised delivery, Frank checked his order and, although peeved at the company's refusal to specify a narrower time frame, arranged to take a day off from work to await his purchase. When the desk had not arrived by 4:20 P.M., he called yet again and was told that the delivery truck was running late and might not arrive before 6:30. At 7:00 P.M., it still had not arrived. Frank demanded that the delivery be rescheduled within a two-hour time period and that he be refunded 20 percent of the price of the desk. Staples complied with his demand.

Acceptable: Dan Treder of Franklin, Michigan, visited the Omni Ambassador East hotel in Chicago in late 1993 for the long New Year's Eve weekend. After his first night, he awoke and discovered that his room lacked hot water in the shower and had no running water in the sink.

The front desk immediately approved a room change. But as he gathered together his belongings, Dan got to thinking: That was no compensation for his inconvenience in having to repack, move his stuff, and unpack anew in another room. He called the manager and stressed that, in an average year, he gave the hotel eight to ten nights worth of business. The manager charged him for only two nights of his four-night stay.

Unacceptable: Ivan Bernstein of Miami Beach checked into the Hyatt in Dallas for a three-day vacation. The hotel was packed with guests attending two conventions headquartered at the hotel. The lines in the restaurant were long. The elevators, while all working, were crowded. Bernstein was furious at the crowding and demanded a reduction of his bill. That demand was unwarranted. If he'd wanted peace and quiet, he should have gone to an inn or a bed-and-breakfast. Everyone knows that major hotels can be chaotic places.

Unacceptable: A man visits an expensive restaurant, gets a steak that's not done to his specification, eats the whole thing anyway, and only then, as the plates are being cleared, demands to see the manager and insists that the price of the steak be removed from his bill. This is patently ridiculous; he has already eaten the steak and is clearly more interested in a financial windfall than satisfaction. Management was not given an opportunity to remedy the wrong, the man cannot justly claim that the pace and smoothness of his dining experience was interrupted, and management will likely be put off by the timing of the complaint.

Acceptable: A man visits an expensive restaurant and orders his steak medium-rare. When he is served it medium-well, he immediately summons the waiter and asks for a new steak done the right way. Since this means that he has to wait while the rest of his party eats their meals, he later suggests that the restaurant give him his dessert free of charge as a way of compensating him for the delay, even appealing to the manager if the waiter says no.

Unacceptable: A woman buys coffee at the drive-through of McDonald's. As she pulls into traffic, she wedges the cup tightly between her legs. The lid pops off from the pressure, and coffee spills out, burning her genitalia. She sues McDonald's because the coffee was too hot.

Acceptable: A woman buys coffee at McDonald's. As she is carrying it to her car, the bottom comes off the cup, spilling the hot coffee out over her hand. She sues McDonald's for serving her hot coffee in a defective cup.

4
The Devil in the Details

The typical consumer gets a bill, quickly eyeballs the total, and—if nothing appears grossly amiss—puts pen to check, scribbling the requested amount.

The typical consumer is a chump.

Elinor, on the other hand, is not, and that is how a quibble over a single line item of seven cents turned into an apparently permanent windfall of $5,239.

Here's what happened:

In the fall of 1993, Elinor was diagnosed with lymphoma and sent for treatment to Johns Hopkins University Hospital in Baltimore. Each month, her visits to doctors, blood tests, medicine, X rays, CAT scans, chemotherapy, and radiation treatments led to garbled, gargantuan bills. Insurance picked up most of the tab, but Elinor still perused the bills with the utmost care. She wasn't about to let Blue Cross/Blue Shield of Maryland get taken by one of the wealthiest hospitals in the nation.

Her first bill, which simply covered consultations with doctors, totaled somewhere in the neighborhood of $4,229. It included one glaringly odd detail: About $540 was claimed by a doctor whom we'll call Dr. Martin Lamme. We're not refusing to disclose his name. Elinor just doesn't remember it because she never met the man. Her doctor's name was Richard Ambinder. His resident was Dr. Sam Denmeade.

So Elinor called the hospital billing clerk and inquired about the bill for the services of the mysterious Dr. Lamme. The clerk explained that Lamme was really a proxy for Denmeade and that it was hospital practice to bill all oncology residents' fees under the name of the chief resident, who was, at that moment, Dr. Lamme.

That practice made no sense to Elinor, who bluntly informed the clerk that she did not pay bills for doctors she had never met.

The clerk didn't budge until Elinor went for the jugular: "Does this mean that if I file a lawsuit regarding my care, Dr. Lamme is a liable party?"

"Uh, uh," the clerk stammered. "Let me check into this and get back to you."

Meanwhile, Elinor phoned Dr. Lamme.

"I'm Elinor Burkett, a lymphoma patient, and you've never seen me, but I just got a bill for your services," she explained. She detailed the hospital policy that allowed this to happen—a policy of which Dr. Lamme was wholly oblivious. And, again, she asked: "Does this mean that you're the one I sue if I have a complaint about Dr. Denmeade's care?"

Weeks later she received a revised bill, with Dr. Denmeade's name on it.

Then came the first bill for laboratory procedures, chemotherapy, drugs, and the like. It, too, included an odd detail: a seven-cent charge for "miscellaneous."

Elinor got back on the phone. "What is miscellaneous?" she asked the billing clerk.

"Well, you know," the clerk responded, "it's miscellaneous stuff."

"What kind of stuff?"

"Miscellaneous stuff."

This was going nowhere. Elinor informed the woman that she did not pay bills for unexplained charges, and that as soon as the seven cents were clarified or expunged, she would be happy to pay the bill in full.

The next month another bill arrived with a new month's charges, plus a running total of what she still owed. Elinor examined the figures closely. The seven cents had not been expunged.

She called the clerk again and began keeping careful records of the date and script of each conversation henceforth. Every month a new and bigger cumulative bill arrived; every month its total reflected the endurance of the seven-cent "miscellaneous" charge. Although the bill ultimately climbed well above $70,000, the hospital never called or wrote Elinor with a clarification of the seven cents.

Blue Cross/Blue Shield of Maryland picked up most of the sum, but more than $5,000 was left to Elinor. It went unpaid. Even after her care ceased, bills for that same sum continued to arrive, and Elinor continued to register her complaint, until she finally wrote the hospital a certified letter.

"I am not failing to pay my bill," she explained carefully. In fact, as she wrote, she had conscientiously paid her physicians' bills promptly, and had even paid her general hospital bills for all years but the one during which she had been charged for "miscellaneous." "I am disputing my bill, and the hospital has done nothing to address that dispute. Until it does, you cannot expect me to pay the bill."

The bills stopped coming. That was more than two years ago. Who can guess the hospital's reasoning? One truth seems abundantly clear: Hospital charges are so horribly inflated and padded that a few thousand dollars means nothing to such establishments.

Even so, Elinor feels that she has struck a blow for health-care reform. At least that's her rationalization on the days when she tries to be high-minded.

The moral of the tale is that no self-respecting consumer should ever pay a bill without reading it—or without challenging unreasonable, fuzzy, or unauthorized charges. Even if you are still mired in the delusion that no one would intentionally try to rip you off, remember that errors are made—and those errors have a strange tendency to be overcharges rather than undercharges.

Who are the worst offenders in bill bloating?

The easiest answer is lawyers—and it is probably not far off the mark. When some attorney tells you that it took him 7.9 hours to prepare a two-paragraph contract, how are you going to argue with him? How do you even know how long it took him?

Maybe you don't, but you should be skeptical, according to our friends who have worked in law firms. Bill padding is so egregious that lawyers even take clients to lunch and then charge them for the time they spent sipping espresso. They bill for the commute between their homes and the courthouse, even when it is shorter than the drive to the office. When you receive your bill, ask to check it against the attorney's office time sheet—not the computerized printout prepared for client billing, but the internal time sheet he fills out. It might not be perfect, but it is likely to be closer to reality than anything else you'll see.

Beware the bills of any business where repairpeople work on commission. Until it got nailed by the California Department of Consumer Affairs in 1992, Sears required all of its mechanics, when working on cars, to make sure they installed or replaced at least $147 worth of parts for every hour they worked. Imagine how reliably their bills reflected the actual state of a car's health. Other mechanics have perpetrated, and continue to perpetrate, similar frauds. Guard against it by telling them up front that you need to authorize any work and that you want to see the parts that were replaced. That's hardly foolproof, but it does cut down on the possibility that you'll be billed for a new carburetor when the old one was left under the hood. If you are charged for work you did not authorize, simply refuse to pay. No one has the right to make you pay for work you did not request.

On the subject of cars, we assume we don't need to remind you of the famous bait-and-switch techniques of automobile dealers, chronicled extensively in magazine exposés and prime-time news shows. But just in case: Always distrust the too-good-to-be-true monthly lease rates that are advertised in newspapers or verbally quoted to you when you go to a dealership.

Frequently, the dealer forgets to mention the up-front deposit. Often, the dealer comes up with arithmetic on the back end that bears no relation to his math on the front end, along with a litany of rationales intended to bludgeon you into submission. Sometimes, these discrepancies are hidden in a contract you've already signed. So before you put your signature anywhere, make sure you understand exactly what you're agreeing to, even if that means obnoxiously asking questions and obtaining assurances a third, fourth, or even a fifth time.

Home remodelers are another major headache, and one of the major causes of complaint to everyone from state attorneys general to the Better Business Bureau. But too often the problem is that you, the consumer, let contractors take you for a ride.

Start with a contract that is extremely explicit. Don't let a contractor get away with saying, "Bathroom remodeling." Make sure the bid includes a list of precisely what the work entails (installation of new fixtures, spackling and painting of the walls, replacement of piping), what kind of materials will be used, and an hourly wage or job rate. If the contractor is supplying materials, ask how those materials will be billed. The usual practice is for the contractor to charge you his price for the materials plus a fixed percentage above that for his trouble. Ask to see his bills for the materials so you can make sure he is sticking to the bargain. If you think the prices he is charging you are outrageous, call his supplier and check the prices yourself.

Above all, never, *ever*, pay the contractor too much money up front. String your payments out so that you always owe him plenty of money. Once he is done, don't give him a red cent until you have inspected the work carefully. Your chances of getting him back to fix something are probably below zero.

If home contractors are devious, health clubs are downright larcenous. Their biggest trick is to lure you into an expensive, pay-by-the-month, three-year contract with the promise that you can break it anytime you want—with only a few conditions attached. Before you believe that and sign on the dotted line, read those conditions carefully.

Frank himself got taken for a ride in a fit of stupidity and laziness when, instead of going through a contract with a fine-tooth comb, he accepted a club worker's verbal summary. She said that if he moved out of Manhattan, even temporarily, and provided proof of his changed address, his membership—and the monthly fee of seventy-five dollars that was being automatically charged to his American Express card—would be terminated immediately. But when he did in fact change addresses and sent the required proof, he got a letter back saying that he was in luck, the health club had affiliates within ten miles of his new location and his membership had been transferred. Meanwhile, the American Express charges continued to come.

Frank ultimately prevailed by whipping off a letter threatening to contact the consumer fraud division of the New York State Attorney General and also lured an investigator from American Express into the scuffle. He threw around words like "bait and switch" and "fraud." Even so, he was duly embarrassed at having been forced to fight in the first place. He should have distrusted the verbal conversation he had when he signed up and read the fine print, which apparently included language about membership transfers.

Warranties merit examination just as close as those given contracts. "One-year warranty" often means for only certain aspects of a product, and not necessarily the features that are costliest and most likely to go on the fritz. A "money-back guarantee" is often as reliable as a Bill Clinton campaign promise. Read carefully. Bring skepticism to the endeavor.

Leave trust and gullibility at home when you go shopping.

GOOD COMPANIES

Lest we be branded unappeasable vigilantes, we would like to acknowledge the existence of a veritable honor roll of fine, upstanding businesses, both large and small, that have demonstrated an exemplary commitment to customer satisfaction. Their standards should serve as both a source of shame and an inspiration for their less distinguished competitors.

Nordstrom. This department store chain's self-proclaimed commitment to service has become an almost annoying refrain, but you know what? Nordstrom makes good on it. When Frank's mother recently bought two twenty-dollar nightshirts there, they arrived not with a simple reminder that she could return them if dissatisfied, but with a Federal Express chit that would enable her to do so in a speedy fashion at the store's expense.

When Frank's sister, Adelle, recently found herself in a Nordstrom on the way to go shopping for a puppy, she asked the women at the concierge's desk if she could use their Yellow Pages to locate nearby animal shelters. They not only assisted her, but also placed calls to the shelters to check if they had puppies of the age, relative size, and color Adelle wanted. Then they validated her parking ticket— even though she had not spent a dime in the store.

Ritz-Carlton. Under a policy called Instant Pacification of Guests, this hotel chain empowers employees to spend up to $2,000 to resolve a guest complaint without special authorization from management. It further requires employees to call a guest back within twenty minutes of a complaint to make sure the problem has been settled. No wonder the hotel chain won the American National Consumer Service Award in 1992.

It should be noted here that other hotel chains maintain similar policies. **Marriott** authorizes low-level employees to spend money to resolve customer complaints without specific approval from higher managers. So does **Four Seasons.** In fact, the doorman at a Four Seasons in Toronto once flew all the way to Washington, D.C., to bring a lawyer a briefcase that had erroneously been separated from the rest of his luggage when it was being loaded into the cab taking him to the airport. For this, the doorman received not a reprimand, but the award of Employee of the Year.

Delta Hotels assures customers a check-in wait of one minute or less—or they get their room for free.

British Airways. In response to customer surveys revealing that their passengers care as much, or more, about what happens before and after a flight as what happens aboard it, this carrier began offering first-class passengers on the New York–London route dinner in a special lounge before boarding and, at the other end, dressing rooms with shower stalls and a clothes pressing service. This airline knows not just how to fly, but how to take off and land.

Home Depot. Proving that total satisfaction is not the purview merely of upper-end service providers, this discount hardware and home improvement chain does not pay employees commissions specifically because it does not want them focusing on shoppers making big purchases at the expense of shoppers making small ones. What Home Depot gives its employees instead is stock in the company, so that they, too, have an investment in happy customers. Home Depot also offers customers free "how-to" seminars. The result: Among the so-called Service 500 companies, Home Depot is number one in ten-year growth in earnings per share of stock.

Chef Allen's. As a matter of course, this North Miami Beach restaurant makes sure that whenever it entertains a party of eight or more, it calls the host the next day to make certain everything was satisfactory.

Brother. (See Chapter 1.)

Scrubadub Car Wash. It promises to wash a customer's car as many times as necessary until the customer feels happy with the results.

5

The Mother of All Consumer Wars

We hate to admit it, but sometimes even the Paul Reveres of consumer terrorism cannot prevail. No matter how skilled, creative, or determined you are, sometimes you buck up against an enemy so entrenched in its own ineptitude, so ossified in indifference, that you cannot force it to budge more than an inch or two.

But defeat comes in varying degrees, and some small form of revenge, along with some picayune compensation, is usually there for the taking. Your challenge as a consumer terrorist is to figure out how to inflict as much pain as you absorbed, because in this way lies sanity, and in this way lies a long-term strategy for getting corporate America to behave.

There is no specific trick to this trade, but rather a general one: Figure out how you can bruise this company, and take off your kid gloves. At the very least, you can gobble up this company's time and burn up its phone lines with your complaints, essentially transforming yourself into a fly that buzzes constantly around managers', service representatives', and executives' heads. At best, you can hit the company where it really hurts—in the bottom line—by exploiting whatever sphere of influence you have to broadcast their sins as loudly as possible.

Our sphere just happens to be a book. The company that installed the windows in Elinor's new home in upstate New York undoubtedly never counted on that, but let this chapter remind them—and corporations like them—that when you enrage a customer, you just never know who that customer is, or what means they have for fighting back.

Elinor and her husband, Dennis, didn't expect to buy Norandex windows. (After all, kids don't exactly lie in bed on long, summer nights and dream of owning specific brands of windows.) But early in the summer of 1995, when they were first starting to build their house, a Norandex salesman we shall call Lloyd Farley appeared on their mountaintop. That was an impressive feat since their mountaintop is twelve miles from the nearest traffic light, up a long dirt road and a 1.6-mile driveway. Lloyd seemed a nice enough guy, a kind of jolly, slightly polished, upscale redneck. Elinor and Dennis were then on a "buy local" binge, and since their new pal Lloyd insisted his windows were on a par with the Andersen windows they'd bought for other parts of the house—but cost less—they plunked down $15,000 and placed their order for nineteen windows—big, huge windows—and a door.

When the Norandex truck pulled up to their house in July, they were ecstatic at their consumer savvy. The windows had been delivered on time. They were carefully crated in enormous wooden boxes. They looked every bit as good as the Andersen windows. The driver didn't have the screens, the handles for the casement windows, or the handles for the door, but that didn't seem to be cause for great worry. Nothing was scheduled to be installed for another month, and surely their pal Lloyd would have the situation rectified by then.

The handles appeared within two weeks, but the screens

did not. No big deal: The approaching season was fall, not summer, and the screens would be of little use for at least another nine months. The windows were the important thing, and they looked gleaming new and gorgeous.

Then the rains came—and the leaking began. First it was just a tiny rivulet, hardly big enough to fill a tin can. "One window out of nineteen isn't so bad," Elinor and Dennis consoled each other. Anyway, they had a ten-year warranty.

Their old pal Lloyd came up to inspect the damage almost the second he was summoned and concluded that someone in the factory had somehow neglected to put the proper amount of silicone on the edge of the glass pane. That sounded to Elinor and Dennis like a reasonable and easy mistake, and they joked with Lloyd that perhaps the window in question was made on a Monday, when the man making it was shaking off a bad hangover from a long weekend.

A crew was promptly dispatched to replace the offending pane. "Good company," Elinor and Dennis congratulated each other. "Prompt service."

Then it rained again—and Elinor and Dennis watched water drip down the insides of the wood frames on two windows. By the morning five more had sprung leaks. This time it took Lloyd longer to return their phone call. This time when Lloyd arrived, cheery and bubbly as ever, Dennis was less amused. Although nuns had spent twelve years drilling the politeness of a quintessential consumer pushover into him, Dennis had by then spent two years with Elinor, who was helping him find what she calls his Inner Yid. He retrieved and latched on to it, threatening to call Norandex corporate headquarters or—more terrifying yet—turn the whole matter over to Elinor.

"Oh, I can take care of her," Lloyd insisted. The construction crew, who were watching the sparring match, shook their heads and mumbled at his arrogance, seeing it for the pure folly it was. They had heard Elinor on the phone handling other consumer disputes. They had seen her in action. And they knew that Lloyd was living very dangerously.

Lloyd also scoffed at Dennis's threat to get Norandex itself involved. "You don't want to call corporate," he said, shoving his foot further into his mouth. "Then your windows will never get fixed."

Lloyd seemed to turn his attention to the matter, spending the next several hours on the telephone. He finally announced that Norandex would magnanimously replace every large window pane in the house for free within ten to fourteen days.

Two weeks later Dennis and Elinor were still waiting for Lloyd to make good on that promise. Dennis tried calling him. He left messages and stomped his feet. No luck. He called Lloyd's boss, who referred him back to Lloyd. By then, the inside panes of two picture windows had cracked and perfect circles of condensation were forming in the center of a third.

Finally, in early November, Lloyd resurfaced in a phone message about delivering the windows the following Saturday. Then he disappeared again for two more weeks before calling to schedule yet another delivery. It was now winter, and Elinor and Dennis's 1.6-mile driveway was covered with snow. "Meet the truck at the bottom of your road and transfer the windows into your four-by-four," Lloyd instructed Dennis.

"What happens then?" Dennis asked. "Do I drive up to the garage and unload all those windows myself?"

Lloyd promised to devise a new plan. A week later he had not done so. Dennis called Lloyd's boss to demand immediate delivery and installation of the windows. He seemed puzzled. The windows were in stock, he admitted, but they could not yet be installed since they were missing some unspecified parts. Dennis did not lose the opportunity to ask whether the missing screens might be with those mysteriously missing parts.

Then, on an extremely snowy afternoon three days before Thanksgiving, Elinor and Dennis heard a feeble knock on their back door. There, against the snow, was the Norandex truck driver, sans truck. As he thawed out, he explained that Lloyd had told him the road would be plowed and a crew on hand to unload the windows. The problem was that Lloyd had made neither arrangement. Another problem was that the truck was stuck in the snow halfway up Elinor and Dennis's driveway, thereby blocking anyone else from using it. The final problem was that the truck didn't contain even half the windowpanes that were needed (and that Lloyd had allegedly ordered).

Lloyd's voice miraculously answered the phone on Dennis's first call. He admitted that the other half of the windows hadn't been ordered. "It must have fallen through the cracks," he said, as if speaking of some removed third party's mistake and taking no responsibility for it. Ever the good ole boy, he insisted he'd already taken care of the matter and guaranteed—not promised, but guaranteed—that on December 5, a local contractor and his crew would meet the Norandex truck at the bottom of the road. They would haul the windows up, install them, and deliver the screens.

Dennis, whose education in consumer terrorism had been accelerated by the experience, was skeptical. He called Lloyd's boss, who admitted that the plan made no sense since his office didn't expect to receive the remainder of the windows for two weeks. He agreed it made no sense to install half the windows on the fifth, so they decided to postpone the appointment and repair the windows on December 14 and 15. A clerk from the Norandex office even called back to confirm the plan. But the contractor whom Lloyd had scheduled for the "guaranteed" date of December 5 didn't learn about—or didn't remember—the change in plan. He showed up as scheduled on the fifth, without the windows.

Finally, shortly before Christmas, four months after the windows had initially been delivered, the great day when they would be replaced and repaired arrived. Only it wasn't so great. One of the windows was missing, one of the replacements was cracked, and another was scratched. By the second day of the work, one of the new panes was forming perfect circles of condensation in its center. No one had any idea where the screens were.

When the crew left, promising to return at some unspecified date with the final three windows and the screens, Elinor and Dennis were freezing from two days of living in a house open, window by window, to the elements. They looked at their lovely new home and almost cried: The woodwork on the windows was still stained from the water. Moreover, with three windows still needing to be replaced, they couldn't finish spackling, sanding, and painting the walls of their living room.

You have never seen nostrils flare as wide as Elinor's did. You have never heard blood boil so violently.

She called up the president of Norandex, figuring he, of all people, would care about his company's utter incompetence. She figured wrong. The president's secretary had clearly received orders to transfer hysterical callers to middle managers, and the middleman assigned to mollify Elinor pledged to have all the repair and replacement work done by the end of January. He would even—praise be to God—expedite delivery of the screens.

Before he could fulfill—or ignore—that promise, one of the new windowpanes cracked. Then eight of the nine windows in the living room began to leak—in new ways, in different places. Elinor's mollifier went missing, pawning her messages off on someone we shall call Henry Andrews, a representative of SNE, the company that actually manufactured the windows as opposed to distributing them. "I don't know what's going on with your house," he said right off the bat, as if suggesting ghosts in the rafters, poltergeists in the beams.

"My house?" Elinor screamed, her cheeks crimson with fury. "Fat chance. The question is, what's going on with your windows?"

That was the pleasant part of the conversation, which grew progressively more combative as Henry kept insisting that SNE's product was impeccable and that the problem had to be Elinor and Dennis's house. Why, Elinor then asked, weren't the Andersen windows leaking? "Fine, what do you want me to say, that Andersen windows are better than ours?" snapped Henry, impressing Elinor with his maturity. "Okay, Andersen windows are better, Andersen windows are better."

Finally, the corporate brains of Norandex and SNE, with their combined IQs of negative two, sent up Lloyd's boss and a local contractor to study the situation. Yup, they concluded, the windows were leaking. As they departed, they pledged to turn the problem over to SNE's engineers. Needless to say, they did not call back. Elinor managed to get a hold of a vice president of Norandex. The engineers proposed weather-stripping the outside of the windows, he explained. Elinor did not accept that proposition. Weather-stripping has a notoriously short life span. Anyway, the repair would change the entire look of the windows. The vice president countered by offering Elinor a full refund—if she and Dennis would return the windows at their own expense.

"Hello?" Elinor said, checking for an intelligent life-form at the other end of the line. "Are you telling me that you want us to pay to have the windows removed and then pay to have new ones installed because you sold us defective windows?" He explained that the Norandex warranty did not include labor. Elinor explained that American juries, packed with consumers, have been known to order major corporations to pay customers millions of dollars for overheating their coffee.

At that point, negotiations broke down and Elinor was passed on to a vice president of SNE whose surname made him sound suspiciously like an anagram of the man she had just been dealing with. A pleasant and civilized guy, he apologized. He responded to phone messages. He offered to have all the windows fixed and to give Elinor and Dennis $3,000 as compensation. He even promised to take care of the missing—and perhaps apocryphal—screens.

The only problem was that he trusted his man Henry to take care of the matter. Henry blew into town from Harrisburg, Pennsylvania, to study the situation firsthand, bringing along Lloyd's boss from Norandex and a local construction worker. Henry sauntered into the house dressed in a $1,000 suit and tasseled Italian loafers, stepping gingerly so as not to smudge them with dust. Gold rings decorated fingers on both of his hands. A gold bracelet dangled from his wrist. His hair was swept up in an immovable bouffant. Elinor found herself wondering if he was, in fact, Leona Helmsley in male drag. Or perhaps Julie Andrews's understudy for *Victor/Victoria*.

"Where are my screens?" asked Elinor, who never minds repeating herself.

Henry smugly produced a box and pulled out eight screens.

"We need ten," Elinor said.

Henry counted the windows, a task for which he needed both hands, and promised to have the two wayward screens sent by UPS.

He did, at least, diagnose the problem in a flash. He pulled off the decorative molding separating the upper windowpanes from the lower, lit a cigarette, and blew smoke at the crack. The smoke wafted up outside the house. Caulk, he concluded. The windows need massive amounts of caulk.

He thought for a moment. "We'll send a crew to do that. I'm pretty good with a caulk gun myself."

"In that outfit?" Elinor said. Henry did not respond.

"What's causing that perfect circle of condensation in that window?" asked Elinor, pointing to the offending pane.

"Oh," Henry replied, "the argon inside between the panes must be excited."

"But argon is an inert gas," Elinor said.

Henry did not respond. Elinor changed the topic.

"And when will the work get done?" Elinor asked Henry.

"Nineteen ninety-eight," Henry responded.

"Not funny," Elinor said. "When will the work be done?"

"Nineteen ninety-eight," Henry responded.

"By then you'll be out of a job, because I'll have bankrupted your company," Elinor said.

"By the end of April," Henry promised.

Then he, too, disappeared into the night. A week later Dennis called the vice president he'd been dealing with at SNE. "Where's Henry?" he asked.

Henry called back saying that he'd been away on Good Friday. He offered no explanation for what he had been doing the other five days.

Finally, he appeared with Lloyd's boss from Norandex and Vince, SNE's service manager in Albany, New York. Donning overalls to protect his Italian designer suit, Henry joined the men in their marathon caulking and their replacement of the final few windows. He also spent the day flicking cigarette ashes on Elinor and Dennis's living room floor.

"What's causing that perfect circle of condensation in that window?" Dennis asked Vince, who was standing next to Henry. Vince looked at the window.

"The inside and outside panes are touching," he responded.

"Where are my screens?" asked Elinor.

"They haven't been delivered yet," said Lloyd's boss, saving Henry. "I'll send them to you next week by UPS."

They used a case of caulk. They inspected every window in the house. They left satisfied that they were rid of Elinor and Dennis.

Less than a week later three windows—windows that had had their panes replaced, that had been caulked and recaulked—began leaking. The vice president at SNE didn't even seem embarrassed when he promised a swift resolution to the problem.

Again he handed it over to Henry. A week later Henry still had not called. The final screens had not been delivered.

Elinor lost her temper. Using every Internet muscle she'd developed during eight years as a reporter, she located the names, addresses, and fax numbers of the leading managers and stockholders of the parent companies of both SNE and Norandex. Then she picked up the phone and called the parent company of SNE.

"Jeffrey Silverman, please." She asked the receptionist for the president of the Fortune 500 company.

"Who's calling?" the woman asked.

"Dr. Elinor Burkett," Elinor responded. The Dr. is not a ruse. Elinor has a Ph.D., which she finds useful primarily in consumer warfare.

The receptionist returned a few minutes later and inquired

as to Dr. Burkett's business. Dr. Burkett explained her business succinctly and was promised that Mr. Silverman would return her call. Of course he did not.

Two days later Dr. Burkett called the receptionist again and reminded her about the unreturned phone call. When the receptionist told her, once again, that someone would call back, Dr. Burkett left a final message: A lawsuit will be filed at 9:00 A.M. tomorrow if I do not receive a response.

Two hours later the director of corporate development phoned from an airport and vowed to explore Elinor's problems and call her the next day.

Overnight, Elinor went to work. Her grievances were boiled down into a thirteen-page memorandum that she faxed to her latest contact; the president of SNE's parent company, Ply-Gem; the president of Norandex's parent company; and various and sundry stockholders, officers, and corporate counsels. She included names, dates, titles, and a dozen well-selected details to demonstrate how thoroughly she had researched the companies. The only facts she left out were about Jeffrey Silverman's romantic history, which she had also uncovered from other newspaper clips.

This time there would be no dilly-dallying, no long, drawn-out negotiation. She gave them seven days to send her a check for $45,000—Dennis's estimate for the cost of replacing all the windows in their house with windows from some other company.

The director of corporate development called promptly the next morning to explain that it would take him several days to research the problem.

"Whatever," Elinor responded. "You've got seven, counting Saturday and Sunday."

The director of corporate development disappeared into that netherworld of incompetents that was SNE. He was replaced by a man sadly out of place in the company: a considerate and professional human being. Tom Volkmann, SNE's newly appointed technical service manager, wasn't overly sympathetic, but Elinor and Dennis needed help more than sympathy. And Volkmann needed training; he was new enough to the company not to understand the depth of its unreliability. Confronted with questions about why the windows needed to be fixed yet again, he began by explaining that Elinor and Dennis's house obviously presented special technical challenges. Elinor asked if technically unchallenged houses experienced no leakage from holes in their windows. That's when Volkmann got on the program.

He arranged for a new set of technicians to fix the windows. He arranged for delivery of the screens. He promised to address the issue of compensation. The end seemed to be in sight.

With some delays.

The long-anticipated screens arrived. They were gold. All the other screens in the house were taupe. Norandex, however, insisted that SNE did not manufacture screens in taupe. Elinor hung up in despair and called Volkmann.

She was back on the phone within an hour. By then Dennis had attempted to install the screen on their custom door unit and it didn't fit. He examined the unit; it wasn't built to specifications. Neither was the door.

Volkmann's technicians arrived and managed to end the leaking in the windows, but they could imagine no way to fit a screen on the jury-rigged door SNE had built. Volkmann's solution seemed simple: Replace the door. But replacing the door meant removing the siding on the house, and since the siding had been factory-stained, there was no guarantee that Elinor and Dennis would be able to match the existing siding if they went this route.

Elinor and Dennis were tired. It was time to try to put an end to the ordeal. They decided they could live with the door: It wasn't perfect, but it worked just fine, and SNE was able to put a sliding screen where the correct, swinging screen was supposed to have been. All that Elinor and Dennis couldn't live with was a lack of compensation. They had more than earned it.

The executives at SNE took out their calculators, put away their pride, and finally presented this offer: a $5,000 apology and a continued, full warranty on any new problems that occurred after this point.

That was, in the scheme of things, chump change.

The real revenge was in the writing.

CRUISING THE NET TO POWER

The key to Elinor's success against Norandex was her uncanny ability to find anything—and anyone—on the Internet, the most valuable tool the consumer guerrilla can wield. What does it get you? Information, and no general ever waged a successful war without knowing everything possible about his enemy.

In dealing with major corporations, Elinor always begins by tapping into the databases of the Securities and Exchange Commission to obtain a current and complete list of the officers and directors of the company she is fighting, as well as the officers and directors of her foe's parent company. (Don't forget: The longer and more convoluted the chain of command, the greater the chance you'll find at least one sympathetic soul.) Elinor's strategy is simple: She uses this information to bother the most powerful, and busiest, people she can. And if they don't respond, she bothers them again and again and again.

The SEC database gives her one other useful type of information: the names and addresses of every individual or group that owns more than 5 percent of the company's stock. Why does she care? Simple: Do stockholders really want to know that their company might be faced with a pesky customer threatening to smear the corporate name from coast to coast? Do they really want to hear from that pesky customer, who promises to write to them daily until her problem is addressed?

The SEC archives are just a start. Elinor also likes to consult both the hometown newspapers of businesses she is battling and the business press (*PR Newswire, Business Wire, The Journal of Commerce*) for up-to-date news she might turn to her advantage. Is the company negotiating a merger? Great, she can recite her tale of woe to the other merging company. Is the business being investigated by the federal government for unfair labor practices or shady bookkeeping? Terrific, she can draw the feds into her battle. Does the president of the company travel the nation giving seminars on the importance of customer satisfaction? Ah, she can ridicule him by offering up snippets of his own speech culled from his own quotes in the press.

That's not all the Internet can do for you. You can tap into TRW credit report and check a company's credit, along with the record of lawsuits against it. Those lawsuits can lead you to fellow consumers who might just share your complaint—and to lawyers anxious to form groups for class-action suits. You can read Standard and Poor's description of your oppressor so you'll have a clear sense of how much the company is worth, a useful piece of information when some corporate honcho tries to accuse *you* of being greedy. If you really get ambitious, search both the SEC archives and biographical databases for details on the lives and salaries of the company's executives. There's no sweeter retort to an accusation of greed than an explanation that you're demanding less than half of 1 percent of the CEO's annual bonus.

Then there is a wide world of special services for the hysterical consumer. "The Wary Buyer" provides news, advice, tips, and rants from a lawyer in Texas named Craig Jordan, whose hobby is helping consumers. Or you can try the guys who have less altruistic motives. Try the Web site of Richard Alexander of the Alexander law firm in California, where you can find articles and other information about how to file complaints. Whittinghill Associates, an Illinois law firm, also maintains a page for consumers, "A Consumer's Bill of Rights," which allows shoppers to share their experiences, sublime or horrendous.

Probably the most complete Web site for would-be consumer guerrillas is "Consumer World," a gateway to thousands of pieces of information, from the names and addresses of corporate officers to the phone numbers of customer service hot lines, from a complete list of the publications of the Federal Trade Commission to a guide to television stations that help aggrieved shoppers. It's a veritable wonderland of consumer alerts, product recall lists, and chat groups where you can post your complaints in public or hone your strategy for attack.

Internet guides to law libraries and other legal resources are important if you are to enter the fray with a hand heavy with information. "LawLinks" bills itself as a resource center for attorneys, legal staff, and consumers. It can lead you through the arcane bylaws of legalese. The "AIMC Consumer Corner" will do so in an even more reader-friendly fashion. Finally, if it is all too much for you—if you simply can't handle the battle yourself—you can log on to the "Outpost" network, where, for a small fee, you can fill out a form and have your complaint sent to everyone who might care about your misery—from state agencies to consumer writers and advocates.

6
Whining Out

If you ask us, and even if you don't, bad service and broken promises in restaurants, hotels, and any kind of travel situation serve up a special kind of hell. It's bad enough to grapple with incompetent dry cleaners and impotent vacuum cleaners on your home turf, but when you encounter problems on terra incognita, or when you're supposed to be having a good time, it's the most debilitating experience imaginable.

Moreover, the definition of unsatisfactory service becomes fuzzy and highly subjective, rendering the task of complaining doubly difficult. Consider restaurants. There is often little way, shy of a charred steak that was ordered rare or a slice of tuna garnished with a wiggling worm, for a restaurant waiter or manager to assess quickly whether your complaint is finicky or fair. Does a restaurant, particularly a finer one, implicitly promise you a seamless and relaxing dining experience or merely a heap o' calories delivered in a relatively expeditious manner?

Or consider hotels. Are they mistreating you if you have to wait ten minutes to check in? If the only room available comes with a bracing view of a solid brick wall, reeks of the last guest's nicotine, or echoes with the sounds of the disco below, should you be compensated for those slim pickings?

Turning to the law for help is a dubious endeavor, because your rights are slim. Airlines are required to compensate you if you've been bumped from a flight because of deliberate over-booking. They must give you at least a pittance if they lose your luggage. And they must provide you access to a seat in a non-smoking section of an airline cabin. That's it. There's no code to compensate you if a baggage handler treats the handles of your leather duffel like footballs or inadvertently rips the wheels off your gliding suitcase. An airline can consign your new Armani suit to fashion oblivion and get away with signing a check that covers only the cost of a replacement from JCPenney.

Restaurants can run afoul of laws mandating cleanliness and prohibiting service of alcohol to minors, but there's no statute preventing them from keeping you waiting for a table an hour longer than you were promised or serving you shrimp that had been frozen longer than most glaciers. Hotels owe you hot water, and that's about it. They almost always provide a phone, but they can charge whatever access fees strike their fancies with virtual impunity.

Still, there are subtle strategies, tiny rebellions and extravagant gestures that can get you what you want, or at least make you feel better. Availing yourself of these can not only help resolve the immediate problem, but can also help reform industries that owe consumers much better treatment than they are accustomed to providing. We advocate a special degree of impatience and a special stamina for griping when it comes to the so-called hospitality industry, because by calling itself that, it is promising so much more than it delivers.

Restaurants
What's so infuriating about bad food and service in a restaurant is that once they have seated you and you are midway through a meal, you're trapped. It's too late to leave for another estab-

lishment. Having ordered the food, you probably already feel liable for the bill. And your lost time is irretrievable.

But you do have some leverage. For one thing, restaurants concerned about a comfortable atmosphere for their patrons are, in general, anxious to mollify any customer peeved enough to cause a public scene. Displaying your willingness to make one is a useful weapon. Better yet, a meal, unlike a piece of clothing, is paid for only after its consumption, so you hold the purse strings until you're completely satisfied.

That was the decisive factor when Frank locked horns with what had previously been his favorite Italian restaurant in the Detroit area back on a Saturday night. Frank and seven friends were celebrating a birthday at Lepanto, a cozy and quietly elegant eatery in the trendy suburb of Royal Oak. The gift-opening started during the lull between dinner and dessert. All but one member had toted presents into the restaurant. The one who had not, Cliff, dashed out to his car to fetch his package.

Immediately, the host appeared at the group's table.

"Can I take this chair?" he asked.

He was told that someone was still using it.

"But I'll bring another right over," he explained.

"In that case, sure," several members of the group assented. The host carried the chair to another group of diners he was in the process of seating.

When Cliff returned, he had no place to sit.

He shuffled his feet for several minutes before Frank testily summoned the host: "What happened to the chair you were going to bring?" The host answered that he didn't have one because a party of people he had expected to leave were still chatting and sipping coffee.

"I can bring over a bar stool," he said.

The group members were regular patrons of this restaurant,

reaching the end of an elaborate and costly meal of veal and martinis, and one of them was now being asked to teeter high above the table and perhaps send a fishing rod down to reach his dessert.

"Oh, no," Frank said. "Let me speak to the manager."

A woman arrived with a strange smile on her face and a strangely jocular attitude.

"They took your chair," she said with a laugh. "That *is* unfortunate."

"No," Frank corrected her. "It's unacceptable."

"Well," she reasoned, "I'm told that you did give them permission."

When Frank and his friends rejected this line of argument, she took another tack: "It's not our fault. Those people at that table over there were supposed to leave."

Voices rose, tempers flared, but never did the manager offer anything resembling a sincere apology, let alone something as significant as a round of desserts on the house. Frank requested to speak to the husband and wife who owned the restaurant, but was told they had left for dinner somewhere else.

"Where did they go?" Frank asked. "Somewhere with chairs?"

Cliff didn't get his own chair for about fifteen minutes, and shared someone else's for the duration of that time. When the bill came, Frank and his friends discussed the proper course of action and quickly reached consensus. They left a $50 tip with the waitress, who bore no responsibility and seemed genuinely mortified, and handed her a note for the owners that included Frank's address and telephone number. They did not pay the $220 bill.

The following morning, a Sunday, Frank's phone rang at 8:30 A.M. When the caller identified herself as one of the restaurant's owners, Frank and his housemate, Rob, readied themselves for an effusive apology. What they got instead was a tongue-lashing about the illegal nature of walking out on the bill. "I could have called the police," the owner said. "And maybe I should have."

The owner scolded Frank and Rob about their behavior, telling them they owed her $220 and lecturing them on the problems and slim profit margins of small business owners. "Those are your problems," Frank said. "I didn't ask you to open a restaurant. But you did, and I went there, and I hardly got my money's worth, and it's absurd that you would expect me to pay the full bill."

Even when Frank informed her that he was a regular customer who had spent hundreds of dollars at Lepanto in the past, and even when the owner acknowledged that the manager recognized him and members of his party as former patrons, the standoff endured.

"What do you want me to do?" she pleaded.

"What do you think you should do?" Frank asked.

"I'll take the cappuccinos off the bill," she offered.

"Oh, jeez, don't put yourself out," Frank answered. "That's not good enough. This wasn't a badly prepared meal. This was a customer without a seat for fifteen minutes in the middle of a meal."

"You're being unreasonable."

"Then call the police. Take me to court."

"What do you want? What will you pay?"

Frank and Rob offered to mail her half the bill, and although she was palpably distraught about it, she accepted, as Frank figured she would. What she wanted was to cover her losses, and something was better than nothing.

As they concluded their conversation, Frank and Rob said,

"The sad thing is that we always loved your restaurant, and now we'll never feel comfortable going there again."

To which she responded: "You'd never be served here again."

Few restaurant disputes are as clear-cut as Frank's, but they can still be won. If you've arrived at a restaurant for an 8:00 P.M. reservation and are still waiting at 8:45 P.M., tell the host or manager that you want to be seated immediately and that you want free drinks for the duration of your wait. If you do this in a loud enough voice, and if you invoke restaurant guidebooks that you'll be happy to contact about your bad experience, you may well prevail, especially because the restaurant management really doesn't want you to leave the eatery and take your money elsewhere.

Other strategies and advice:

1: If you're staying at a fine hotel in the same city, and even if you're not, tell the restaurant's management that you are eager to go back to the concierge there and vividly describe your bad experience, warning him not to send other hotel guests to the restaurant in the future.

2: Shout that the colleagues in your firm frequent this restaurant, but that you will instruct them not to in the future. So long as your complaint is absolutely legitimate, a little fictive pressure is fair game. After all, how many of the excuses they give you for delayed meals and botched drink orders do you really think are wholly truthful?

3: If your waiter or waitress is horrendous, reflect that in the tip. Many customers are afraid they'll look cheap if they leave only 5 or 10 percent of the bill as a tip, but sometimes that's all that's warranted, and sometimes that's the only way an errant serviceperson will learn his or her lesson. Just remember not to punish waiters and waitresses for mistakes that clearly belong to the kitchen or management. That's simply mean and unfair.

(For a handy-dandy, speedy way to evaluate service from waiters and waitresses, see the clip-and-copy tip-scoring chart at the end of this chapter.)

4: If you order a dish that you find unappetizing, even if the mistake lies more in your ordering than in the restaurant's preparation of a dish, you can almost always get the restaurant to bring you a new, different selection free of charge, so long as you express your displeasure right away, and not after you've consumed three-quarters of the dish.

5: You should always remain on the lookout for any instance when a restaurant falls short of specifically stated goals, and you should make them compensate you for it. When Randy Friedberg, a lawyer in New York, took his girlfriend to Tavern on the Green, he did so in part because the restaurant had advertised a Valentine's Day special including a $10,000 Bulgari ring in one of the Cracker Jack boxes distributed to every couple.

According to a 1995 article in the *New York Times*, only after his meal was Randy told that the promotion had been canceled. So he took the famous restaurant to court, and was indeed awarded full reimbursement for his meal that night.

6: You should also remain on the lookout for extra charges in your bill that you weren't apprised of or that are flatly ridiculous, such as wine corking fees that weren't clearly advertised. One customer told the *New York Times* that he was charged a miscellaneous eighteen dollars by a restaurant because it had to push two tables together to accommodate his party. Items like these can almost always be successfully disputed, because most restaurant managers realize how petty they will seem if they insist on payment. The main reason the charge is there in the first place is that restaurants know most customers will be too shy or blissed-out on Cabernet to whine.

7: Make sure restaurants are following rules about nonsmoking areas and sanitary conditions. If they seem not to be, let the manager or owner know that you suspect this, and that you know which authorities you should contact. This can trigger instant cooperation with any beef you might have.

8: Don't assume that lower-priced restaurants are less likely to be responsive to your dissatisfaction. In fact, if these restaurants belong to chains, you're in the best situation possible, because they have corporate parents that can afford small losses for future customer satisfaction. These corporations care about that satisfaction because the whole point of a chain is to engender habit in customers happy to find a trusted, known eatery everywhere they go.

We've been told that an extra long wait on line at McDonald's almost always yields free French fries if a complaint and request are made, and that dissatisfaction with one kind of sandwich invariably yields a free coupon for another.

In the same month that Frank had his horrible experience at Lepanto, a friend had a terrific one at the decidedly more downscale Chili's, a TGI Friday's–like chain heavy on the burgers and ribs. This man had made reservations for a party of eight and was kept waiting for an hour. He made his displeasure and his frequent patronage of Chili's well known, but didn't even have to suggest a particular remedy. When the meal was over, management told him that it was on the house.

Hotels

Elinor frequently fantasizes that she is a magnet for bad service and stupid clerks, that her consumer karma guarantees that no interaction can be pacific. Even on those days when she convinces herself that she is indulging in paranoia, she still cannot escape the belief—the certainty, in fact—that she will never have an acceptable experience at a hotel. Her travels are an unbroken series of bathrooms without towels, nonworking telephones, missing room service menus, and forgotten phone messages. But she reached the nadir one Sunday night when she got stuck at O'Hare Airport in Chicago. Tired and cranky after three days traipsing around the Midwest in 103-degree temperatures, all she wanted was a decent bed, a working television, and an air conditioner that would cool her body to something approaching 98.6.

Instead, she got the Days Inn O'Hare South—at eighty-nine dollars for the night. After a twenty-five-minute wait to check in and a four-mile hike to her room (okay, so maybe it was just the length of six city blocks), she became testy when she looked at a ceiling pockmarked with ill-patched water stains. Her testiness mounted when the front desk simply didn't answer the phone. But the bed was comfortable and the television worked, so she swallowed her frustration, turned down the thermostat, took off her clothes, and waited for the sweet touch of frigid air.

Fifteen minutes later, the air remained at the same sticky 84 degrees. She called the front desk. Someone finally answered.

"Oh, yes, we're having some problems with the air-conditioning," the clerk acknowledged.

"Why didn't you warn me before you took my eighty-nine dollars and sent me to my room?" Elinor inquired.

"Oh, we just found out a little while ago," the clerk stammered.

"How long ago?" Elinor responded.

"When did you check in?" the clerk asked.

Even baked, Elinor was not that stupid. She asked to speak to the manager.

"There is no manager available on weekends," the clerk said.

"What do you do if you have an emergency?" Elinor inquired.

"We call the local police," the clerk responded dryly. She then offered to knock 10 percent off the price of Elinor's room. Elinor did not believe that solution sufficient. She offered to let Elinor check out. Elinor suggested that sending a single woman out into one of the less savory neighborhoods of Chicago at 9:30 P.M. did not seem a wise idea. The clerk insisted no further alternatives were available.

Elinor, of course, managed to find one. She spent the night in her sauna and, in the morning, asked to see her credit card slip, then summarily tore it up. Before she departed, she left the still-absent manager a note explaining her course of action. She also left her phone number and suggested that the manager might want to call her.

The manager never did. And Elinor never had to pay the bill.

Refusing to pay is an excellent strategy when the circumstances warrant it, but there are other ways to make sleeping away from home a less risky endeavor.

1: Especially in tourist areas, hotels are notorious for over-booking, so it is not entirely uncommon to arrive at a hotel thinking you have a reserved, guaranteed room to find yourself on the street. If that happens to you, demand that the hotel arrange for you to have a room at a comparable nearby hotel, pay for at least one night of your stay there, forward your phone and fax messages, pay for a cab to your new lodgings, and offer you an upgrade on your next stay with them. Few establishments will refuse these demands.

   If yours does, and if you reserved your room with a credit card, call the bank that handles it. Visa, for example, has a travel and entertainment resolution fund it offers for just such situations.

2: To minimize the possibility that you will be left roomless, turn the tables on hotels by forcing them to acknowledge your reservation as a contract. It's simple. When you place your reservation, send or fax the hotel a confirmation of what you were told on the phone—the price of the room, the kind of room, whatever amenities you were promised. Note on your confirmation that any disputes about the contract shall be heard by the courts of *your* hometown and state. Take a copy of the confirmation letter with you when you check in. You are unlikely to be mistaken for a dishrag.

3: Don't let any establishment that pretends to offer hospitality get away with filling your bathroom with pathetic rect-angles of cloth that feel no better than sandpaper. Perhaps we're overly demanding, but we believe that every American has an inalienable right to a decent towel. If your hotel doesn't offer one, go out and buy a decent towel and deduct the price of it from the bill. And don't forget to leave the towel when you depart. After all, you're not trying to get something for free, you're just trying to make sure both you and the next guy don't abrade your skin.

4: Declare war on absurd hotel phone rates: *Never* use a hotel long-distance service. (Come on, business travelers, we know that your company is paying the bill, but everyone needs to work on this together.) If it weren't so impractical, we'd tell you to boycott hotel telephones altogether, since the rates charged border on extortion. The hotel industry insists that profits from phone service are actually dwindling, but they still make almost $2 billion a year charging us a buck to call out for a pizza.

5: Okay, so some nights you can't resist diving into the minibar. Who can blame you when a hotel dangles chocolate at $3 a bite in front of you and dares you not to break it open? We don't expect that you'll be able to resist 100 percent of the time. But at least don't let the hotel get away with charging you $3.75 for a can of Coke. Keep track of what you eat, and before you check out, stop at the local 7-Eleven and replace it. See what that does to their 300 percent profit margins!

6: Try to stay at a hotel that guarantees satisfaction. That's not as unusual as you might think, even if you're not a big-budget traveler who can afford to stay at a place like the Four Seasons, which we applaud under "Good Companies." **Embassy Suites**, for example, offers suites rather than mere rooms and guarantees high-quality accommodations and good service. They back that guarantee up with a promise to refund your money with no hassles.

Airlines

Getting there used to be half the fun, but these days it's not even a quarter or an eighth. Airlines demand that you arrive thirty minutes early and then keep you waiting on a stuffy airplane on the runway for two hours before you finally take off. They give you a plastic bag with a stale sandwich, eight potato chips, and a cookie, and call it "bistro service," as if any bistro on the Right Bank, the Left Bank, or the fringes of Boise, for that matter, could lure a customer with such fare. They lose your luggage, ask you to estimate the value of the belongings inside, then balk at the sum and demand receipts for two-year-old bras and four-year-old skirts.

We won't bore you with torrid tales of airline horrors. If you've ever left the ground, you have your own. Airlines are begging for a whipping and, unfortunately, we don't have many clever suggestions for how to deliver it short of insurrection. We admit that during those long hours when we've been marooned on planes sitting on the runway without taking off we've fantasized about such open rebellion. Imagine organizing the passengers to stand up and shout, "Freedom now!" And we'd love to see someone launch a campaign to demand that airlines back up their on-time claims with something more meaningful than lies. Braniff used to offer cold cash for every minute the plane was late taking off. We can be reasonable; we'd settle for frequent-flier miles instead. If just one airline were to adopt such a program, the rest will fall like flies before our invincible rage.

But none of these fantasies, sweet as they are, helps you much when you are trying to get to Des Moines from Chicago. So here are a few modest proposals:

1: Hold airlines to their promises. If your flight promises lunch and you are served a lilliputian roll with cardboard-hard turkey and an ancient orange, complain. Snacks are not meals. Demand compensation either in the form of a voucher for a meal at the airport or a discount on your next flight.

2: If you want a decent meal, order a vegetarian or kosher entrée when you make your reservation. The portions are bigger and the food is tastier.

3: Memorize the rules for compensation if you are bumped from a flight, and demand your full due: If you are bumped but they can still get you to your destination within an hour of your original arrival time, you get nothing. (On the other hand, if you get there that fast you probably are doing better than you would on most flights.) If you are bumped and your arrival is delayed for two hours, you are owed 100 percent of the value of your ticket up to $200, and your ticket is still good. If your arrival is delayed four hours, the price doubles to $400.

4: Don't let airlines strand you during four-hour delays. If you are pushy, they will buy you a meal, book you onto another carrier, or find another way to get you to your destination. If it's late at night, demand a hotel room to boot. And don't let them get away with our favorite outrage (so many outrages, so little space): refusing to offer any sort of accommodation for passengers whose trips are originating where the delay occurred. You paid for your ticket. Let them pay for their incompetence. Most important, if you can make other arrangements that will get you to your destination faster, do not let the original airline charge you a cancellation or rescheduling penalty.

5: Don't accept even minor inconveniences and lapses in service without compensation. If you're flying across the country, you have the right to a pillow and a blanket—and the airline should compensate you if they run out. If you asked for an aisle seat when you made your reservation and were pushed into a middle seat when you boarded the plane, you were given inferior service. In fact, if you show even the slightest inclination that you will make a scene or abandon the airline in the future, you will be offered discount coupons or first-class upgrades with alacrity.

CAB-IAL PURSUIT
A Clip-and-Copy Formula for Tipping Taxi Drivers

Roadsmanship

-2	-1	0	1	2
Evil Knievel	Joseph Hazelwood	Okay	Mario Andretti	Captain Kirk

Cleanliness

-2	-1	0	1	2
Calcutta	New York City	Okay	Minneapolis	Singapore

Sound Effects

-2	-1	0	1	2
Tunisian belly dancing	Anthrax	Okay	Rush Limbaugh	NPR

Decor

-2	-1	0	1	2
National Geographic	*Martha Stewart Living*	Okay	*Highlights*	*Metropolitan Home*

Politeness

-2	-1	0	1	2
Pro wrestler	Ice hockey player	Okay	Bowler	Cricketer

English

-2	-1	0	1	2
Marcel Marceau	Dan Quayle	Okay	Arnold Schwarzenegger	William Safire

BONUS POINTS:

Cuts off limousines	+1
Cuts off limousines discharging dignitaries	+2
Stops within 12 inches of curb	+2

SCORING and TIPPING:

13 to 17 points: 20 percent tip	0 to 5 points: 5 percent tip
8 to 12 points: 15 percent tip	-5 to 0 points: No tip
5 to 8 points: 10 percent tip	Below -5 points: Don't pay fare

THE WAITING GAME
A Clip-and-Copy Formula for Tipping Waiters

Fashion

-2	-1	0	1	2
Yasser Arafat	Fidel Castro	Okay	Louis Farrakhan	Mikhail Gorbachev

Personality

-2	-1	0	1	2
Autistic	Schizophrenic	Okay	Manic-depressive	Obsessive-compulsive

Etiquette

-2	-1	0	1	2
Roseanne	Murphy Brown	Okay	The Nanny	Mary Tyler Moore

Efficiency

-2	-1	0	1	2
Sisyphus	Narcissus	Okay	Odysseus	Hercules

BONUS POINTS:

Raises eyebrows at wine selection	-4
Cologne overpowers aroma of food	-2
Confesses that bouillabaisse is gastronomic apocalypse	+4

SCORING and TIPPING:

8 to 12 points: 20 percent tip
4 to 7 points: 15 percent tip
0 to 3 points: 10 percent tip
-5 to 0 points: 5 percent tip
-6 to -9 points: No tip
Below -9 points: Don't pay the bill

7
Bill of Rights

If you're one of those naive souls whose response to getting pushed around by merchants is to huff and puff and declare, "But I have rights," you're in trouble. You have some rights, but not many. The system is stacked against the consumer by a horde of lobbyists who are paid extremely well to make sure that you live at the mercy of big business. Like Don Quixote, you can end up tilting at windmills if you don't know precisely the right pressure to apply and when to apply it. So, when you consider your legal rights, think of yourself as a member of a tiny guerrilla band battling a well-equipped army of 500,000. You have to know the terrain better than your enemy—and make sure you fire each shell with deadly accuracy.

Some terrains are more advantageous to you than others, because most consumer regulations are state or local. While in most states, for example, you have no special protection against a store's charging you more for an item than the price indicated on the shelf, in Michigan, that behavior earns you ten times the difference between the price marked and the price charged—and they have to give you the money on the spot.

We thus urge readers to contact their local consumer protection authorities (the addresses of state agencies are listed in Appendix B) for information on state and local laws. But here are a few general principles applicable nationwide.

If You Buy Something and Are Dissatisfied

First, check your warranty, which may well limit your options. A warranty is a contract, so the company that provides it is legally obliged to follow its terms. The problem is, so are you, which means that you might be forced to allow a manufacturer the option of repairing your product, rather than replacing it, which means that you might be liable for the cost of shipping a refrigerator motor to them. All warranties have expiration dates, but remember: If you report a defect during the warranty period and the product was not fixed properly, your warranty coverage continues for that problem even after the expiration date.

Don't ever let a merchant get away with telling you that you have no warranty. All products come with "implied" warranties, as required by the laws of every state and the Uniform Commercial Code. The only time you have no warranty is when a product is clearly marked for sale "as is." Furthermore, "as is" sales are illegal in many states, including Kansas, Maine, Vermont, Mississippi, West Virginia, Maryland, Massachusetts, and the District of Columbia.

The most common type of implied warranty is a warranty of merchantability, which means that the merchant promises that the product he sells you will work. If a merchant suggests that a product is appropriate to a given function—a heater will warm a small room well, for example—that product is also covered under a so-called warranty of fitness for a particular purpose. That means that if the heater leaves your small room the temperature of your refrigerator, you have the right to a full refund. The length of coverage for an implied warranty varies from state to state.

If a company does not resolve a warranty problem to your satisfaction, you have the right under the Magnuson-Moss Act to sue for damages and whatever else the court is willing to award you.

If You Buy Something with a Credit Card and Are Dissatisfied

You are clearly in a stronger position than if you paid with cash, but don't think that you can wash your hands of a bad transaction by calling your credit card company and canceling the charge for a defective product or unacceptable service. Some credit card companies are extremely amenable to helping resolve disputes, but legally you can only dispute a charge of more than fifty dollars, and then only if the business you dealt with was within one hundred miles of your home. If you meet both conditions, don't tarry. The Fair Credit Billing Act requires you to file your dispute in writing within sixty days of receiving the relevant credit card bill. Your credit card company must resolve the dispute within ninety days.

Shopping by Phone and by Mail

You have two major protections if you consume from home. First, the postmaster general frowns upon mail order fraud and will go to bat for you if you're its victim. Second, the Federal Trade Commission Mail or Telephone Order Rule protects you from companies that take your money but delay sending your purchases. The law requires a company to ship your order within thirty days of the processing of your charges or within the length of time specified in its advertisement. If they cannot comply with that obligation, they must send you a notice offering you the option of agreeing to an extension or receiving a prompt refund. (The time limit is extended to fifty days if you applied for credit to pay for the purchase.)

Consumers should also note that federal law limits a company's ability to bother you endlessly with phone calls from persistent salesmen. Under the Telemarketing Sales Rule, it is illegal for a company to call you if you've already said you don't want to be bothered. Furthermore, unless you specifically agree, they are guilty of abusive telemarketing practices if they call you before 8:00 A.M. or after 9:00 P.M. your time. Your state attorney general can prosecute under this statute, and we encourage you to ask him to do so.

Shopping at Home

If you buy something at home or at the equivalent of a Tupperware party, you have special rights. The Federal Trade Commission Cooling-Off Rule guarantees you three days to cancel a purchase made in such settings as long as you spent more than twenty-five dollars. There are dozens of exceptions, including cars bought from another individual, crafts fairs, and the like, but cite this law loudly and clearly if you are denied a refund within that time limit.

Travel

Most of the regulations—what few exist—are covered in Chapter 6. But you need to know about a few more. If you get bumped from a flight on which you have a reservation and aren't happy with the settlement offered by the airline, you do not have to accept it. Although those payments are mandated by the government, the U.S. Supreme Court has affirmed your right to sue the airline instead. It might not be worth it, since you can recover only out-of-pocket damages—nothing for loss of business or vacation time. But you never know when this ruling might come in handy

Laws against fraud and misrepresentation can often help you fight a travel promoter. If you've been ripped off by a cruise line or tour agency, contact the attorney general's office in the state where the business is located (see Appendix B for addresses). If you purchased your ticket or trip by mail, complain to the U.S. Postal Inspection Service's regional office where the business is located. Your local postmaster can give you the address.

Laws about health and safety can help you fight a cruise line that has made your life miserable. If the problem is safety, call the U.S. Coast Guard's consumer hot line 800-368-5647. Report unsanitary conditions on cruise ships to the U.S. Public Health Service, Vessel Sanitation Program, 1015 North America Way, Room 107, Miami, FL 33132, 305-536-4307. You might never lodge these complaints, but threatening to do so packs a wallop.

Miscellaneous

Often the greatest challenge is to find a law that can be made to cover your problems. For example, many states and localities have laws against gender discrimination that you can use as weapons against dry cleaners that charge more for women's clothing than men's, hair salons that make women pay more for the same haircut than men, and even bars that offer cheap drinks to females on "ladies night." Cleaners insist that women's clothing is more expensive to press than men's clothing, but don't believe them. A shirt is a shirt, and if your state has gender discrimination laws, you don't have to pay more just because the buttons are on the left. If you just want to get a cheaper rate, claim that the shirts belong to your husband. If you want to make a stink, file a discriminatory practices complaint.

Furthermore, if you are a member of a group that is offered specific antidiscrimination protection because of age, race, ethnicity, or sexual orientation, and there is any hint that that status has detracted from your service, complain to your local authorities on that basis, or threaten to do so, which could make a dogmatic merchant heel promptly.

A CAUTIONARY TALE

Sometimes, however, the law is irrelevant. Even when you have right on your side, the price of pursuing it is sometimes unacceptably high. Obviously, we don't advocate rolling over and playing dead when you are ripped off. But we also don't advocate making the pursuit of justice a lifetime—or life-destroying—crusade when the damage is meager. Sure, you have your honor to defend. But remember: There's no shame in retreat, as long as it is well-calculated. We offer as a morality play in the uselessness of legal remedies the amazing story of Debbie, Bill, Emma, and the moving company.

Debbie and Bill are a thirtysomething New York couple who in 1995 bought a brownstone in Brooklyn just five blocks from their apartment. Hiring United Van Lines to haul their belongings such a short distance seemed absurd, so they decided to pack themselves. They asked around among friends for a small company with a truck and some muscle.

The company they heard about was no longer hauling, but the manager there recommended a guy from Brooklyn named Richie. At 5'4" and 130 pounds, Richie seemed too small to carry their furniture up and down three flights of steps. But even when they pointed to their wall of books—sixty or seventy boxes worth, at least—he was not discouraged. "Five men and a van and we're done in no time at all," Richie insisted, pointing to his van.

Anyway, the price—just $700—was so right that they didn't even bargain with Richie. In fact, it was so "reasonable," as they called that unbelievable bid, that they even offered to pay him more money to finish their packing. "No problem," he said once more, accepting their $350 deposit and agreeing to come by the day before the move to fill the remaining boxes.

Richie and Anthony showed up right on time, but that was the final reasonable occurrence of their encounter. Anthony packed voraciously: trash on the floor, dirty glasses, the filled garbage pail. And when he sealed the cartons, he mummified them, spending long minutes encasing them in yard after yard of tape. At first, Richie was tolerant. "He's a moron," he said. "But he's okay." An hour or so later his attitude changed. "I'm never working with a moron like you again," he snapped at Anthony. Still later in the day, he summarily fired the man, ordering him to leave the house.

After Anthony departed, Richie took up position by Debbie and Bill's bay window and sat there for a good long while.

"What's going on?" Debbie asked after half an hour.

"I'm exhausted," Richie responded. "This is killing me."

Debbie, who had a managerial position at a not-so-modest newspaper, was not cowed. "But you're a mover," she said, "and we have to be out of this apartment by tomorrow night."

"But all these books," he said. "I've never seen so many books."

"But we *really* have to be out by tomorrow night," Debbie pressed, cuddling one-year-old Emma in her arms and looking at the five boxes of books Richie had packed, compared to the hundreds of volumes still on the shelves.

Richie exploded: "Me, me, me, that's all you think about. All you care about is yourself. What about me? From the beginning you never cared about me."

Debbie could think of no reply likely to advance her cause, and acquiesced as Richie left, vowing to finish up the packing while his men began the hauling the following morning.

Only Richie didn't show up the following morning. Instead,

two merchant marines on leave appeared at the door with a small van. Their progress was glacial, because they had to take turns sitting in the van, guarding it against a parking cop.

It was getting dark by the time they finally began loading the prepared boxes into their absurdly small van. They proclaimed exhaustion and their desire to stop for the day. Bill urged them on. "But we'll be at it until three A.M.," they insisted. "And Richie only paid us to work until two P.M."

They finally called Richie, then sheepishly approached Bill to ask for a favor. "Richie is threatening to fire us because we haven't finished the job," they said. "He says we must have been sitting on our butts all day. Can you call and tell him we've been working our tails off?"

Bill was sympathetic to their plight. He knew Richie had been right in the first place when he said they'd need five men and a large truck.

"Pay them what you owe and we'll worry about the rest later," Richie told Bill when he called.

"What rest?" Bill demanded. Richie was suddenly protesting the amount of work involved in the move, as if Debbie and Bill had somehow tricked him. Richie demanded triple-time to finish the work. Bill countered that he wouldn't pay Richie another cent until the job was done.

By then Bill was desperate. His family's possessions were strewn between the old apartment and the new house, the beds were disassembled and Emma needed someplace to sleep. He'd been begging the merchant marines to take the beds over to the new place, but they kept moving books and kitchen appliances. Finally, he got in his car and drove over to the new house to urge them to take just one more load. They came back, helped Bill carry the bed outside to the van, and offered to fill it up one more time before they drove over to the new house.

Bill sighed with relief.

Then Richie appeared at the house. "Look, Richie," Bill said. "I'm not paying you until you finish the job."

"We'll see about that," Richie said as he left to go downstairs, promising to send one of the men up to take out the rest of the bed.

The door slammed. "Boy, what a sucker," Bill heard one of the merchant marines laugh. His heart stopped. He knew. He just couldn't believe it. Ten minutes passed. Fifteen minutes. Twenty minutes. He descended the stairs haltingly. Richie's car was gone. The van was gone. Everyone was gone—along with the bed, the stereo, the computer, the television, and the bike. Meanwhile, there were still loads and loads of unmoved belongings in the apartment.

Bill got little solace from the police. "We're not going to get in the middle of a labor-management dispute," they told him over the phone.

"This isn't even a discussion about moving," Bill said. "This is theft. They've taken my stuff and vanished."

The police finally deigned to come over. Emma promptly threw up on their shoes. After some prodding, they paid a visit to Richie, who admitted that he was "holding" Bill and Debbie's possessions until they paid him.

"This can be simple or it can be complicated," they told Bill. "You want these possessions back, right? If you file charges, and this seems to fit the definition of theft, things get complicated. Your stuff becomes evidence, and we might have to hold it. You'll probably have to go to court.

"You know what I'm saying here. I'm not trying to lead you anywhere. But this guy says you owe him money. Do you agree with that? He says you were going to pay him seven hundred dollars and now that's not enough."

"I don't owe him anything," Bill insisted. "He didn't finish the job."

The cops shook their heads and departed. The next day, they returned with Richie and a van filled with Bill and Debbie's things. Again, the cops tried to negotiate with Bill.

"He says he finished three-quarters of the work, so he should get three-quarters of the money," they said.

"Not a cent," Bill replied. He agreed only to reimburse Richie for the cost of the boxes. The cops consulted with Richie.

"That's okay with him but he wants to reserve the right to sue you," they said.

Bill laughed for the first time that day.

That night, Bill, Debbie, and Emma camped out on the floor in their new home. In the morning, they studied the Yellow Pages and found the most reputable company possible. "No problem," the movers said when they described the amount of work left. "Three hundred and fifty dollars."

They came right over. Even when they upped their estimate to $600, Debbie and Bill didn't panic. The men were large. They had a big truck. They moved everything at lightning speed and placed each item carefully in the right room in the new house. Debbie and Bill were relieved. They forked over cold cash.

Then a policeman appeared at the door. "Is that your stuff on the truck?" he asked Bill, pointing to the belongings not yet in the house.

"Yes," Bill replied, hesitantly.

"Well, you better get it off fast, because this truck is about to be impounded."

"Impounded?" Bill stammered.

The list of complaints was endless: The truck driver had no license to drive, the serial number had been filed off the engine block, the inspection sticker was doctored, and the registration belonged to a different—stolen—truck.

As the police tow truck drove up, Bill and Debbie scurried to unload their possessions onto the sidewalk. The moving men had disappeared.

For a minute—just one minute, actually—Bill and Debbie thought about calling the police and reporting the latest rip-off. Then they thought about their computer languishing in some evidence locker for six months and understood what they must do—and what you, too, must do if you are to avoid the trap of becoming so intent on consumer victory that you wind up paying too dear a price for it.

They forgot about their rights and chalked the $600 up to experience.

TO SUE OR NOT TO SUE

Suing is a terrific idea if you're a lawyer, or if making lawyers rich is your idea of fun. For the rest of us, it is expensive and time-consuming.

But if you've yelled, written letters, gone up the chain of command, and exhausted every strand of creativity in your body, you either have to put up or shut up: Eat your loss or go to court.

Conventional wisdom suggests that you start with small-claims court. That's a reasonable suggestion since small-claims court will give you a hearing date within weeks of your filing, is never costly (filing fees are usually between fifteen and thirty dollars), and hearings rarely last longer than thirty minutes. You can call witnesses and present evidence, but you don't have to worry about legalese or the traditional rules of evidence.

That's the good news, but—inevitably—there's a downside.

First, representing yourself is always risky, especially in states where lawyers are allowed in small-claims court. Sure, you can hire a lawyer, too, but that almost defeats your purpose. Besides, the other guy can probably afford more legal muscle than you can.

Second, winning doesn't mean collecting. In almost half of small-claims-court judgments, the defendant either can't or won't pay—so you have either wasted your time or you have to go back to court to get your opponent's wages garnished or property seized.

Third, when you file in small-claims court, you give up your right to appeal, but the defendant does not.

Fourth, you have to file in a court where the company—or one of its subsidiaries—does business. So you can wind up spending a bucket of money on travel and hotels for very little return.

Finally, the amount you can recover is pretty limited. In Arkansas, it's only $300, while in Massachusetts and New York, it's $5,000.

If you still want to go ahead, consult your local telephone book under the municipal, county, or state government headings for small-claims-court offices. The clerk of the court will usually guide you through the filing.

As for regular civil courts, it is certainly true that customers with complaints as seemingly dubious as injury from hot coffee have reaped tremendous windfalls. But for every such victory, there are scores of defeats that cost starry-eyed consumers the moon. We absolutely recommend consulting a lawyer if thousands of dollars are in dispute and your case is extremely strong. Otherwise, this should be the method of last resort. Threatening with civil court will not scare many merchants. They know that, particularly in the current political climate, they pack more legal artillery.

8

Declaration of Independence

Although this book serves as the clarion call formally heralding the long overdue dawn of consumer terrorism, make no mistake: The first bright blasts of battle have already begun flaring on the horizon. The advance is under way, visible in the brave missions of a few bold guerrillas who have approached the fortress of corporate America, taken a battering ram to its gates, weakened its ramparts, and pointed the way for the rest of us.

Consumer rebellion wasn't even a distant fantasy when John Barrier of Spokane, Washington, marched into the vanguard of the war against corporate greed and pigheadedness by devising a potent way to punish a bank he felt had mistreated him. John had been a thirty-year customer of Old National Bank when he pulled into the parking lot of one of its branches in October 1988 to pay a visit to his broker there. As he left, an attendant tried to charge him a sixty-cent parking fee, so Barrier returned to the bank to ask the receptionist to validate his ticket. She refused, saying that he had not conducted a transaction while inside the bank.

John cashed a check, then returned to the receptionist with proof of his transaction. She again refused to validate his ticket, parroting an apparent bank policy of "no deposit, no validation." Wondering if part of her attitude had to do with the way he was dressed—he was wearing shabby, dirty clothing—he assured the receptionist that he had substantial business with the bank and urged her to call his own banker at another branch of Old National to verify this. She responded that if he wanted to make the call, there was a pay phone nearby. His appeal to the branch manager elicited no more sympathy or cooperation.

John then drove to his own branch to tell his banker that if he did not receive a call of apology from someone in the bank's management by the next day, he would withdraw all his funds and deposit them with a competitor, Seafirst Bank. When the call didn't come, he drove to the nearest Seafirst and wrote a check for $1 million, the amount of money he had formerly kept with Old National.

"If you have $100 or $1 million, I think they owe you the courtesy of stamping your ticket," he later explained to reporters.

Those reporters wrote brief stories about the quirky incident, but passed it off as an isolated oddity. No one seemed to consider the possibility that Barrier was a portent of things to come.

Roxanne Logan of Waterford, Michigan, outside Detroit, has similarly been written off as an anomaly, even though she won herself a story in *Money* magazine and an interview with Frank by extolling her consumer savvy, which she estimates increased her 1994 income by $2,500 in rebates from stores, restaurants, and service providers. Roxanne is a formidable opponent.

She once complained to a hamburger chain that a hard object in one of its patties had chipped her tooth, and elicited $1,750 toward present and future dental work. She then protested that her dentist hadn't anesthetized her properly and won a 50 percent reduction in her $400 bill. She regularly receives $75 or even $150 coupons from airlines whose performances disappoint her and free meals from restaurants whose food she finds unappetizing. According to *Money*'s profile of her, she even got $50 from a Days Inn because the bathroom was dirty. (And when she wasn't happy with that profile, with which she cooperated by freeing up hours of her time, she complained and suggested she receive a year's free subscription, which *Money* sent her, albeit with a letter saying that it was not an apology, but rather a "token of our appreciation.")

John Banzhaff III, a professor of law at George Washington University, poses a more serious threat to corporate harmony because he actually trains his students to turn the law into a sledgehammer that will bludgeon merchants into postures of abject humiliation. His motto, emblazoned on his stationery, is "Sue the Bastards." His hobby, noted on his curriculum vitae, is "Suing the Bastards." He promises students who take his course on legal activism that they will learn both "legal judo" and "guerrilla law." But he, too, has been unable to grab the public imagination and channel it into a weapon that can strike terror into the hearts of American business.

That task fell to neither a millionaire nor a law professor, but to thirty-eight-year-old Jeremy Dorosin, the owner of a scuba equipment shop who turned an arguably unextraordinary dispute with the Starbucks coffee chain into a cause célèbre that became a roar heard and a fire felt in corporate boardrooms across the nation. The Godzilla of disgruntled customers was profiled by dozens of newspapers, including the *New York Times*, and on at least a half dozen television news programs, from *Hard Copy* to the *CBS Evening News*.

We would never advocate Dorosin's approach to consumer terrorism, which cost him $20,000 and yielded no comparable financial return. But for Americans who have been cheated, abused, and forced to listen to hours of Muzak while on infinite hold, Dorosin stands as a martyr to the cause of consumer justice, the man who served potent notice to businesses nationwide of the damage that one peeved patron can do.

"I think large companies are increasingly going to be on guard because they'll realize that the consequences of an angry customer can be worse than they ever imagined," Jeremy says of the results of his crusade. "I think the sense of immunity corporations feel is beginning to change. This idea that you can treat the customer any way you want is beginning to fade away.

"They think that the longer they can let it drag on, the more likely the customer will just go away. But what about the monster? What about the one who just won't quit? There are a lot of people like that, and I happen to be one of them."

The creation of that monster began in April 1995 when Jeremy visited a branch of Starbucks in Berkeley, California, to purchase an Italian espresso machine. He says that the steam pump soon went on the fritz, and that he returned the machine to the store, getting a loaner while repairs were being made on his own unit. He liked the loaner so much that he went back to the store to purchase one as a wedding gift for a friend.

His first stabs of apprehension came when he examined the box, which seemed slightly tattered. He says that a store clerk assured him that boxes sometimes sustained damage when being shipped from Europe and that there was no need for concern. In any case, this machine was the last one in stock. So Jeremy went ahead and purchased it.

When he got to the checkout counter, he asked the cashier for the free half-pound of coffee that the store normally provides with major machine purchases. According to Jeremy, the cashier refused to grant him even a free cappuccino, bluntly stating: "You get nothing." Starbucks has acknowledged the cashier's error.

But Starbucks disputes Jeremy's next bone of contention. He says that when the friend to whom he gave the machine as a wedding present opened it, she saw that it was rusted and a part was missing. She concluded that it must be used. "This was really embarrassing to me," Jeremy says, explaining that the woman was a special friend who was getting remarried and beginning a new chapter in her life after a horrible battle with cancer. "I figured: She thinks I got some piece of shlock out of my garage."

Jeremy's anger was all the greater because he knew first-hand how hard some businesspeople work to mollify dissatisfied customers. For the seven years he'd operated Scuba Town in Walnut Creek, near his home of Pinole, California, he had maintained one clear policy: Whenever a customer expressed legitimate disappointment over even the smallest problem, he'd offer them something for free as an apology—even if it cost him hundreds of dollars.

"Sure, there is the type of customer who does scams all the time," he adds. "But does that constitute the majority of people who patronize a business? Absolutely not."

So when he found out about the rust on his gift, Jeremy went back to his local Starbucks to complain. Dissatisfied with the response, he then appealed to company management in San Francisco. Still unappeased, he directed his wrath to managers at the chain's headquarters in Seattle, suggesting that, as an apology, Starbucks send his friend a model of the nicest machine it stocked. That machine, they told him, cost more than $2,000. He suggested the next nicest model, worth $450. Again, they balked, although they offered to refund his money and send him two new espresso makers of the kind he had bought—one for him, one for his friend. Jeremy did not believe that offer compensated him for his trouble and his embarrassment both in the store and with his friend.

So he decided to take his battle public in a flamboyant—and expensive—fashion. He bought an advertisement that ran in the Northern California edition of the *Wall Street Journal* on May 5 that read: "Had any problems at Starbucks Coffee? You're not alone. Interested? Let's talk." The ad also provided a toll-free number. This was followed by bigger, more expensive ads in the entire Western edition of the *Wall Street Journal*. This ended up costing him about $8,000, he says. The news media took notice, and soon Jeremy's story was spreading like wildfire through the land.

It also forced Starbucks to take Jeremy more seriously, but the gestures of appeasement it provoked did nothing to placate the Californian. The company ultimately sent him two new espresso machines, two pounds of coffee, a steaming pitcher, condiment shakers, cups, saucers, and a thirty-dollar refund. He refused to accept delivery. He was irate that the merchandise came only after the second of his five ads. For him, it was a classic case of too little, too late. By that point, he says, he was beyond wanting specific recompense. He wanted the world to know how Starbucks had treated him, and he wanted more extravagant displays of apology.

Rooting around in his mind for a demand, he first came up with this: a two-page ad in the *Wall Street Journal* in which Starbucks would express its remorse for selling him a used machine. Starbucks refused, saying that such an admission would be a lie, because the machine it sold was not used. Jeremy then suggested that Starbucks establish a center in San Francisco for runaway children. Starbucks again refused, even though one independent consultant, Ron Zemke of Performance

Research Associates, told the *New York Times:* "If I were Starbucks, I'd be in San Francisco right now with a shovel, digging the foundation."

Jeremy never got what he wanted from Starbucks, but he got something else: He hit a sensitive national nerve among consumers fed up with feeling like businesses didn't care about their feelings and their disappointments. By June of 1996, he had received 6,000 calls on his toll-free line, and the charges for those, plus his expenses from responding to inquiries, added another $12,000 to the money he had already spent on newspaper ads.

In addition, he received an offer to become the head of public relations for another growing coffee and food company. A master stroke on that company's part, and yet another embarrassment to Starbucks.

Ironically, Jeremy was not a consumer terrorist-in-waiting before his encounter with Starbucks. In fact, he says he can count few serious disputes with any businesses before that epic clash. But his conflict with Starbucks tapped into a deep wellspring of unease he harbored about the changing service-scape of American society, an unease he shares with millions of his fellow citizens.

Gone are the days when small stores staffed by proud owners tend to customers with concern. Instead, minimum-wage employees staff the counters of enormous corporate Goliaths that make any single customer feel like a puny David. In this case, however, the peons are not doing battle with the giants. "I don't think customers complain too much," he says. "I think they complain too little."

As for Starbucks, its manager of customer relations during Jeremy's dispute, Barbara Reed, offered the *New York Times* this reflection in June 1995: "I think it's great that people yell and scream, but we have a responsibility to all our customers, and this one has gone too far." She said that surrendering to Jeremy's escalating demands "would be a ridiculous waste of money to appease one ego." And she asked: "If we can't settle this, where are we as a nation?"

Where are we indeed? The answer is clear: We're at a point where Americans from all walks of life—of all races, religions, and political creeds—are declaring their independence from bad products and worse service. A point where customers are no longer content to lick their wounds, but are becoming intent on exacting revenge. A point where companies must listen longer, harder, and with considerable generosity to rabble-rousers at their gates, barbarians or not. We're in the era of consumer terrorism.

What John Barrier, Roxanne Logan, John Banzhaff III, and Jeremy Dorosin have shown us—and what we have shown you—is the existence of an alternative to resignation and despair. That alternative is battle. You now have the ammunition you need. Go forth, take aim, and fire.

Appendix A: Answers to C.A.T. Test

Answers to Part I

1: Give yourself 100 points if you answered (e), because the sob story is guaranteed to speed you toward your goal and the embarrassment etched on the maître d's face will be priceless. If you answered (a), take 80 points, both for getting your table and wreaking revenge on the restaurant with your insect alarm. Answering (c) wins you 60 points, because a bar tab is something, but not all that much. Answering (b) nets 40 points, because you at least denied the restaurant your money. Selecting (d) nets 20, and suggests that you should go into victim counseling.

2: The best answer, worth 100 points, is (b), because while the balance of power between doctor and patient tilts woefully in the former's favor, the magazine gambit just might work. Next best, at 80 points, is (c), because the coughing fit is terrific revenge, even better theater, and a promising strategy for clearing out the office. Next comes (e), worth 60 points, because it's sensible, combining the relief of the bath with the hope of better luck next time. Answer (a) gets you 40 points, because at least it gets you out of the office and ends your immediate captivity. Answer (d) is worth only 20 points, because we can't believe you want to get naked in public.

3: And the winner is . . . answer (a), worth 100 points, because it's sensible and it'll work; Frank did precisely that once. The runner up . . . answer (d), worth 80 points, because you're demanding something sensible and it will also work. Answer (e) is next, and nets 60 points, because while suing is rarely an efficient option in such minor situations, at least you're throwing a tantrum. Answer (c) is worth 40 points, because plastic is, after all, safer than glass. And answer (b), at 20 points, pegs you as hopeless, a would-be consumer terrorist who can't even muster the courage to carry a squirt gun.

4: The best answer, worth 100 points, is (d), because it gets you your stereo and eliminates any inconvenience you suffered. Next best, worth 80 points, is (c), because, while inconvenienced, you accomplish your mission. The 60-point answer is (e), because while you don't get your stereo, you feel better and have taken out some measure of revenge by disrupting store business. Selecting (a) gives you 40 points, because you at least attempted some form of retribution, although the Better Business Bureau is next to worthless. And at the bottom of the heap, worth 20 points, is (b), because you have let them make a chump of you.

5: The terrorist's crown—and 100 points—goes to those who chose option (b), which nets you a new coat plus some extra booty, and is a more plausible outcome than you might assume. A runner-up prize—and 80 points—goes to those who chose (c), which reveals a consumer terrorist in training. Those who chose (d) get 60 points, because they salvaged something useful out of their disappointment, while those who selected (a) get 40 points, because they showed some sense. If you answered (e), you get only 20 points, because you're nuts.

6: It's a hard choice between (c) and (d)—the choice between immediate gratification of your hunger and the comfort of eating in your hotel room—but we think you should give yourself 100 points if you chose (d), since hotel food is clearly superior to airport fare. Give yourself 80 points if you answered (c), since you showed spunk and creativity. Answer (e), worth 60 points, shows you're moving in the right direction, but the demand is too vague. Answer (b), for 40 points, is a wise precaution, but does little to improve service on airlines. If you sunk so low as to select (a), at 20 points, you are probably hopeless and should simply stop flying—or consuming.

7: Award yourself 100 points if you answered (d), since what is the driver going to do if you shove twenty dollars in his face and get out of his cab? Not far behind, worth 80 points, is answer (e), since it gets you out of a sticky situation without further injury. Answer (c), at 60 points, is a pretty poor choice since you are in Chicago, where public officials are not notoriously pure. Answer (a), at 40 points, might be gratifying, but be real: We're trying to teach you to behave like a consumer terrorist. If you selected (b), worth 20 points, you should definitely not go to Chicago.

8: Our real favorite is (a), since it is dramatic, gratifying, and money-saving, but since most people don't have pickup trucks or friends willing to cart around refrigerators all day, the top award of 100 points goes to (d). The next best response, worth 80 points, is (b), since it accomplishes your goal with no added expense. If you answered (a), give yourself a pat on the back for vengeance and flair, but only 60 points, since your time and inconvenience need to be protected. Answer (c) might, in fact, be productive since manufacturers are often more responsive than dealers, but it will take time, so is worth only 40 points. Choosing (e) brings you only 20 points, since vitamin supplements are even more expensive than vegetable crispers.

Answers to Part II

Each correct answer is worth 100 points.

1: The correct answer is (b). According to the Fair Credit Billing Act, you can dispute only charges over fifty dollars. Moreover, such charges must be made within one hundred miles of your home.

2: The correct answer is (d). The Federal Trade Commission Cooling-Off Rule provides that amount of time for you to cancel purchases made in your home or at a location that is not a permanent place of business, as long as the purchase is for more than twenty-five dollars.

3: The correct answer is (e). Federal Aviation Administration regulations require a carrier to pay you $200 if they bump you but can reschedule you to depart within *two* hours of your original time of departure. The amount rises to $400 if you are further delayed. Carriers will frequently offer you a voucher for a free flight instead. You have the right to demand the cash or to sue for a higher sum.

4: The correct answer is (b). Sex discrimination in public places is outlawed under federal law.

5: False. Under the Uniform Commercial Code, any product not sold "as is" comes with an "implied warranty of merchantability," which means that it is supposed to work.

6: The correct answer is (c). In most locales, landlords are required to refund your deposit plus standard bank interest.

At a 5 percent annual interest rate, that amount would approximate $1,650, answer (b), but interest rates, and local laws, vary.

7: The correct answer is (d). The Federal Trade Commission Mail or Telephone Order Rule requires companies to ship your order within the time stated in its ads, or within thirty days of the processing of your charges if no time is promised. If they are unable to do so, the company must send you a notice offering you the option of further delay or cancellation.

8: The correct answer is (b). While your limit of liability with credit cards if $50, with ATM or debit cards, that limit rises to $500 after forty-eight hours.

If you received a perfect score of 1,600 points, you are probably time-sharing a brain with the authors of this book and clearly need to read no further. Give it to a friend or write to HarperCollins and demand a refund.*

1,400–1,580 points: You're pretty close—a consumer vigilante, at least. Skim the book and demand a 50 percent refund from HarperCollins.*

1,000–1,380 points: You're ready to bear arms, but need some instruction in using them.

600–980 points: You're not hopeless, but you need this book.

*This is a lesson in reading the fine print. Who do you think you're kidding? Actually, we're kidding. HarperCollins will not refund one red cent.

300–580 points: You need this book *real bad*.

Under 300 points: You need this book *so desperately* that you should send HarperCollins a contribution of twenty dollars in gratitude for saving your consumer life. Or you can make the check out directly to **Frank Bruni** and **Elinor Burkett**.

Appendix B: Consumer Resources

The addresses and phone numbers listed in this appendix, while accurate at the time the book went to press, may have changed. The authors apologize for any such changes.

Government consumer periodicals available from the Consumer Information Center in Pueblo, Colorado, can also be downloaded onto your computer from catalog.pueblo@gsa.gov. If you want to check on product safety or current recalls, use a gopher to take you to the Consumer Product Safety Commission site on the Internet (Gopher to cpsc.gov).

Most of the information in the following section is taken from the Consumer's Resource Handbook produced by the United States Office of Consumer Affairs.

State, County, and City Government Agencies

Government consumer protection offices and state attorneys general often investigate or mediate complaints, prosecute offenders of consumer laws, and provide educational materials to the public. They can also give you information on what laws apply to various consumer problems in your state.

The following is a list of the state offices as assembled by the U.S. government. Don't forget to also contact your local authorities—either the county consumer affairs office or the county district attorney—and/or your city officials.

Alabama
Consumer Affairs Division
Office of Attorney General
11 South Union Street
Montgomery, AL 36130
205-242-7334
800-392-5658 (toll free in AL)

Alaska
The Consumer Protection Section in the Office of the Attorney General has been closed.

American Samoa
Consumer Protection Bureau
P.O. Box 7
Pago Pago, AS 96799
011-684-633-4163
011-684-633-1838 (fax)

Arizona
State Offices
Consumer Protection
Office of the Attorney General
1275 West Washington Street
Room 259
Phoenix, AZ 85007
602-542-3702
602-542-5763
Consumer information and
complaints: 800-352-8431 (toll free
in AZ)

Consumer Protection
Office of the Attorney General
402 West Congress Street, Suite 315
Tucson, AZ 85701
602-628-6504

Arkansas
Consumer Protection Division
Office of Attorney General
200 Tower Building
323 Center Street
Little Rock, AR 72201
501-682-2341 (voice/TDD)
800-482-8982 (toll free voice/TDD
in AR)

California
California Department of
Consumer Affairs

400 R Street, Suite 1040
Sacramento, CA 95814
916-445-1254 (consumer
information)
916-522-1700 (TDD)
800-344-9940 (toll free in CA)

Office of Attorney General
Public Inquiry Unit
P.O. Box 944255
Sacramento, CA 94244-2550
916-322-3360
800-952-5225 (toll free in CA)
800-952-5548 (toll free TDD in CA)

Bureau of Automotive Repair
California Department of
Consumer Affairs
10240 Systems Parkway
Sacramento, CA 95827
916-255-4300
800-952-5210 (toll free in CA—auto
repair only)

For Los Angeles:
Consumer Protection Division
Los Angeles City Attorney's Office
200 North Main Street
1600 City Hall East
Los Angeles, CA 90012
213-485-4515

Consumer Protection, Fair
    Housing, & Public Rights Unit
1685 Main Street, Room 310
Santa Monica, CA 90401
310-458-8336
310-458-8370 (Spanish hot line)

Colorado

Consumer Protection Unit
Office of Attorney General
1525 Sherman Street, 5th Floor
Denver, CO 80203
303-866-5189

Connecticut

Department of Consumer
  Protection
165 Capitol Avenue
Hartford, CT 06106
203-566-2534
800-842-2649 (toll free in CT)

Antitrust/Consumer Protection
Office of Attorney General
110 Sherman Street
Hartford, CT 06105
203-566-5374

Delaware

Division of Consumer Affairs
Department of Community Affairs
820 North French Street, 4th Floor
Wilmington, DE 19801
302-577-3250

Economic Crime and Consumer
  Protection Division
Office of Attorney General
820 North French Street
Wilmington, DE 19801
302-577-2500

District of Columbia

Department of Consumer and
  Regulatory Affairs
614 H Street, N.W.
Washington, DC 20001
202-727-7120

Florida

Department of Agriculture and
  Consumer Services
Division of Consumer Services
407 South Calhoun Street
Mayo Building, 2nd Floor
Tallahassee, FL 32399-0800
904-488-2221
800-435-7352 (toll free in FL)

Consumer Litigation Section
Office of the Attorney General
4000 Hollywood Boulevard, Suite
  505-South
Hollywood, FL 33021
305-985-4780

Georgia

Governors Office of Consumer
  Affairs
2 Martin Luther King Jr. Drive,
  S.E.
Plaza Level–East Tower
Atlanta, GA 30334
404-651-8600
404-656-3790
800-869-1123 (toll free in GA)

Hawaii

Office of Consumer Protection
Department of Commerce and
  Consumer Affairs
828 Fort Street Mall, Suite 600B
P.O. Box 3767
Honolulu, HI 96812-3767
808-586-2636

Office of Consumer Protection
Department of Commerce and
    Consumer Affairs
75 Aupuni Street
Hilo, HI 96720
808-933-4433

Office of Consumer Protection
Department of Commerce and
    Consumer Affairs
3060 Eiwa Street
Lihue, HI 96766
808-241-3365

Office of Consumer Protection
Department of Commerce and
    Consumer Affairs
54 High Street
Wailuku, HI 96793
808-243-5387

Idaho
Office of the Attorney General
Consumer Protection Unit
Statehouse, Room 119
Boise, ID 83720-1000
208-334-2424
800-432-3545 (toll free in ID)

Illinois
Governors Office of Citizens
    Assistance
222 South College
Springfield, IL 62706
217-782-0244
800-642-3112 (toll free in IL)
(Only handles problems related to
state government.)

Consumer Protection Division
Office of Attorney General
100 West Randolph, 12th Floor
Chicago, IL 60601
312-814-3000
312-793-2852 (TDD)

Department of Citizen Advocacy
100 West Randolph, 13th Floor
Chicago, IL 60601
312-814-3289
312-814-3374 (TDD)

Regional Offices
Carbondale Regional Office
Office of Attorney General
626A East Walnut Street
Carbondale, IL 62901
618-457-3505
618-457-4421 (TDD)

Champaign Regional Office
34 East Main Street
Champaign, IL 61820
217-333-7691 (voice/TDD)

East St. Louis Regional Office
Office of Attorney General
8712 State Street
East St. Louis, IL 62203
618-398-1006
618-398-1009 (TDD)

Granite City Regional Office
Office of Attorney General
1314 Niedringhaus
Granite City, IL 62040
618-877-0404

Kankakee Regional Office
Office of Attorney General
1012 North Fifth Avenue
Kankakee, IL 60901
815-935-8500

LaSalle Regional Office
Office of Attorney General
1222 Shooting Park Road, Suite 106
Peru, IL 61354
815-224-4861
815-224-4864 (TDD)

Mt. Vernon Regional Office
Office of Attorney General
3405 Broadway
Mt. Vernon, IL 62864
618-242-8200 (voice/TDD)

Peoria Regional Office
Office of Attorney General
323 Main Street
Peoria, IL 61602
309-671-3191
309-671-3089 (TDD)

Quincy Regional Office
Office of Attorney General
523 Maine Street
Quincy, IL 62301
217-223-2221 (voice/TDD)

Rockford Regional Office
Office of Attorney General
119 North Church Street
Rockford, IL 61101
815-987-7580
815-987-7579 (TDD)

Rock Island Regional Office
Office of Attorney General
1710 Third Avenue
Rock Island, IL 61201
309-793-0950
309-793-6839 (fax)
309-793-0953 (TDD)

Consumer Protection Division
Office of Attorney General
500 South Second Street
Springfield, IL 62706
217-782-9020
800-252-8666 (toll free in IL)

Waukegan Regional Office
Office of Attorney General
12 South County Street
Waukegan, IL 60085
708-336-2207
708-336-2374 (TDD)

West Frankfort Regional Office
Office of Attorney General
607 West Oak Street
West Frankfort, IL 62896
618-937-6421

Dupage Regional Office
Office of Attorney General
122A County Farm Road
Wheaton, IL 60187
708-653-5060 (voice/TDD)

Indiana
Consumer Protection Division
Office of Attorney General
219 State House

Indianapolis, IN 46204
317-232-6330
800-382-5516 (toll free in IN)

Iowa
No listing given

Kansas
Consumer Protection Division
Office of Attorney General
301 West Tenth
Kansas Judicial Center
Topeka, KS 66612-1597
913-296-3751
800-432-2310 (toll free in KS)

Kentucky
Consumer Protection Division
Office of Attorney General
209 Saint Clair Street
Frankfort, KY 40601-1875
502-564-2200
800-432-9257 (toll free in KY)

Consumer Protection Division
Office of Attorney General
107 South Fourth Street
Louisville, KY 40202
502-595-3262
800-432-9257 (toll free in KY)

Louisiana
Consumer Protection Section
Office of Attorney General
State Capitol Building
P.O. Box 94095
Baton Rouge, LA 70804-9095
504-342-9638

Maine
Bureau of Consumer Credit
   Protection
State House Station No. 35
Augusta, ME 04333-0035
207-582-8718
800-332-8529 (toll free in ME)

Consumer and Antitrust Division
Office of Attorney General
State House Station No. 6
Augusta, ME 04333
207-626-8849 (9:00 A.M.–1 P.M.)

Maryland
Consumer Protection Division
Office of Attorney General
200 St. Paul Place
Baltimore, MD 21202-2021
410-528-8662 (9:00 A.M.–3:00 P.M.)
410-565-0451 (DC metro area)
410-576-6372 (TDD in Baltimore area)

Eastern Shore Branch Office
Consumer Protection Division
Office of Attorney General
201 Baptist Street, Suite 30
Salisbury, MD 21801-4976
410-543-6620

Western Maryland Branch Office
Consumer Protection Division
Office of Attorney General
138 East Antietam Street, Suite 210
Hagerstown, MD 21740-5684
301-791-4780

Massachusetts

State Offices

Consumer Protection Division
Department of Attorney General
1 Ashburton Place
Boston, MA 02103
617-727-8400
(Information and referral to local
consumer offices that work in
conjunction with the department of
attorney general.)

Executive Office of Consumer
    Affairs and Business Regulation
One Ashburton Place, Room 1411
Boston, MA 02108
617-727-7780 (information and
referral only)

Western Massachusetts Consumer
    Protection Division
Department of Attorney General
436 Dwight Street
Springfield, MA 01103
413-784-1240

For Boston:
Mayor's Office of Consumer Affairs
    and Licensing
Boston City Hall, Room 613
Boston, MA 02201
617-635-4165

Michigan

Consumer Protection Division
Office of Attorney General
P.O. Box 30213

Lansing, MI 48909
517-373-1140

Bureau of Automotive Regulation
Michigan Department of State
Lansing, MI 48918-1200
517-373-4777
800-292-4204 (toll free in MI)

For Detroit:
City of Detroit
Department of Consumer Affairs
1600 Cadillac Tower
Detroit, MI 48226
313-224-3508

Minnesota

Consumer Services Division
Office of Attorney General
1400 NCL Tower
445 Minnesota Street
St. Paul, MN 55101
612-296-3353

For Minneapolis:
Minneapolis Department of
    Licenses & Consumer Services
One C City Hall
Minneapolis, MN 55415
612-673-2080

Mississippi

Director, Office of Consumer
    Protection
P.O. Box 22947
Jackson, MS 39225-2947
601-354-6018

Bureau of Regulatory Services
Department of Agriculture and
    Commerce
500 Greymont Avenue
P.O. Box 1609
Jackson, MS 39215-1609
601-354-7063

Missouri
Office of the Attorney General
Division of Consumer Protection
P.O. Box 899
Jefferson City, MO 65102
314-751-3321
800-392-8222 (toll free in MO)

Consumer Protection Division
Office of Attorney General
P.O. Box 899
Jefferson City, MO 65102
314-751-3321
800-392-8222 (toll free in MO)

Montana
Consumer Affairs Unit
Department of Commerce
1424 Ninth Avenue
Box 200501
Helena, MT 59620-0501
406-444-4312

Nebraska
Assistant Attorney General
Consumer Protection Division
Department of Justice
2115 State Capitol
P.O. Box 98920
Lincoln, NE 68509
402-471-2682

Nevada
Commissioner of Consumer Affairs
Department of Commerce
State Mail Room Complex
Las Vegas, NV 89158
702-486-7355
800-992-0900 (toll free in NV)

Consumer Affairs Division
Department of Commerce
4600 Kietzke Lane, B-113
Reno, NV 89502
702-688-1800
800-992-0900 (toll free in NV)

New Hampshire
Consumer Protection and Antitrust
    Bureau
Office of Attorney General
State House Annex
Concord, NH 03301
603-271-3641

New Jersey
Division of Consumer Affairs
P.O. Box 45025
Newark, NJ 07102
201-504-6200

Deputy Attorney General
New Jersey Division of Law
P.O. Box 45029
124 Halsey Street, 5th Floor
Newark, NJ 07101
201-648-7579

New Mexico
Consumer Protection Division
Office of Attorney General

P.O. Drawer 1508
Santa Fe, NM 87504
505-827-6060
800-678-1508 (toll free in NM)

New York

New York State Consumer
    Protection Board
99 Washington Avenue
Albany, NY 12210-2891
518-474-8583

Bureau of Consumer Frauds and
    Protection
Office of Attorney General
State Capitol
Albany, NY 12224
518-474-5481

Bureau of Consumer Frauds and
    Protection
Office of Attorney General
120 Broadway
New York, NY 10271
212-416-8345

New York State Consumer
    Protection Board
250 Broadway, 17th Floor
New York, NY 10007-2593
212-417-4908 (complaints)
212-417-4482 (main office)

Regional Offices

Binghamton Regional Office
Office of Attorney General
59-61 Court Street, 7th Floor
Binghamton, NY 13901
607-762-1013

Buffalo Regional Office
Office of Attorney General
65 Court Street
Buffalo, NY 14202
716-847-7184

Plattsburgh Regional Office
Office of Attorney General
70 Clinton Street
Plattsburgh, NY 12901
518-563-8012

Poughkeepsie Regional Office
Office of Attorney General
235 Main Street
Poughkeepsie, NY 12601
914-485-3920

Rochester Regional Office
Office of Attorney General
144 Exchange Boulevard
Rochester, NY 14614
716-546-7430

Suffolk Regional Office
Office of Attorney General
300 Motor Parkway
Hauppauge, NY 11788
516-231-2400

Syracuse Regional Office
Office of Attorney General
615 Erie Boulevard West
Syracuse, NY 13204-2465
315-448-4848

Utica Regional Office
Office of Attorney General

207 Genesee Street
Utica, NY 13501
315-793-2225

For New York City:
New York City Department of
    Consumer Affairs
42 Broadway
New York, NY 10004
212-487-4403

Bronx Neighborhood Office
New York City Department of
    Consumer Affairs
851 Grand Concourse
Room 913
Bronx, NY 10451
718-590-6006

Brooklyn Neighborhood Office
New York City Department of
    Consumer Affairs
1360 Fulton Street, Room 320
Brooklyn, NY 11216
718-636-7092

Ms. Isabel Butler, Director
Queens Neighborhood Office
New York City Department of
    Consumer Affairs
120-55 Queens Boulevard
Room 301A
Kew Gardens, NY 11424
718-261-2922

North Carolina
Consumer Protection Section
Office of Attorney General

Raney Building
P.O. Box 629
Raleigh, NC 27602
919-733-7741

North Dakota
Consumer Fraud Section
Office of Attorney General
600 East Boulevard
Bismarck, ND 58505
701-224-3404
800-472-2600 (toll free in ND)

Ohio
Consumer Frauds and Crimes
    Section
Office of Attorney General
30 East Broad Street
State Office Tower, 25th Floor
Columbus, OH 43266-0410
614-466-4986 (complaints)
614-466-1393 (TDD)
800-282-0515 (toll free in OH)

Office of Consumers' Counsel
77 South High Street, 15th Floor
Columbus, OH 43266-0550
614-466-9605 (voice/TDD)
800-282-9448 (toll free in OH)

Oklahoma
Office of Attorney General
Consumer Protection Division
4545 N. Lincoln Boulevard
Suite 260
Oklahoma City, OK 73105
405-521-4274

Department of Consumer Credit
4545 N. Lincoln Boulevard
Suite 104
Oklahoma City, OK 73105-3408
405-521-3653

Oregon
Financial Fraud Section
Department of Justice
1162 Court Street N.E.
Salem, OR 97310
503-378-4732

Pennsylvania
Bureau of Consumer Protection
Office of Attorney General
Strawberry Square, 14th Floor
Harrisburg, PA 17120
717-787-9707
800-441-2555 (toll free in PA)

Office of Consumer Advocate-
    Utilities
Office of Attorney General
1425 Strawberry Square
Harrisburg, PA 17120
717-783-5048 (utilities only)

Bureau of Consumer Protection
Office of Attorney General
1251 South Cedar Crest Boulevard
Suite 309
Allentown, PA 18103
215-821-6690

Bureau of Consumer Services
Pennsylvania Public Utility
    Commission

P.O. Box 3265
Harrisburg, PA 17105-3265
717-783-1470 (out-of-state calls only)
800-782-1110 (toll free in PA)

Bureau of Consumer Protection
Office of Attorney General
919 State Street, Room 203
Erie, PA 16501
814-871-4371

Bureau of Consumer Protection
Office of Attorney General
132 Kline Village
Harrisburg, PA 17104
717-787-7109
800-441-2555 (toll free in PA)

Office of the Attorney General
Professional Building
P.O. Box 716
Ebensburg, PA 15931
814-949-7900

Bureau of Consumer Protection
Office of Attorney General
21 South Twelfth Street, 2nd Floor
Philadelphia, PA 19107
215-560-2414
800-441-2555 (toll free in PA)

Bureau of Consumer Protection
Office of Attorney General
Manor Complex, 5th Floor
564 Forbes Avenue
Pittsburgh, PA 15219
412-565-5394

Bureau of Consumer Protection
Office of Attorney General
214 Samters Building
101 Penn Avenue
Scranton, PA 18503-2025
717-963-4913

For Philadelphia:
Economic Crime Unit
Philadelphia District Attorney's Office
1421 Arch Street
Philadelphia, PA 19102
215-686-8750

Puerto Rico
Department of Consumer Affairs
   (DACO)
Minillas Station, P.O. Box 41059
Santurce, PR 00940-1059
809-721-0940

Department of Justice
P.O. Box 192
San Juan, PR 00902
809-721-2900

Rhode Island
Consumer Protection Division
Department of Attorney General
72 Pine Street
Providence, RI 02903
401-274-4400
401-274-4400, ext. 2354 (TDD)
800-852-7776 (toll free in RI)

Rhode Island Consumers' Council
365 Broadway
Providence, RI 02909
401-277-2764

South Carolina
Consumer Fraud and Antitrust
   Section
Office of Attorney General
P.O. Box 11549
Columbia, SC 29211
803-734-3970

Department of Consumer Affairs
P.O. Box 5757
Columbia, SC 29250-5757
803-734-9452
803-734-9455 (TDD)
800-922-1594 (toll free in SC)

State Ombudsman
Office of Executive Policy and
   Program
1205 Pendleton Street, Room 308
Columbia, SC 29201
803-734-0457
803-734-1147 (TDD)

South Dakota
Division of Consumer Affairs
Office of Attorney General
500 East Capitol
State Capitol Building
Pierre, SD 57501-5070
605-773-4400

Tennessee
Division of Consumer Protection
Office of Attorney General
450 James Robertson Parkway
Nashville, TN 37243-0485
615-741-3491

Division of Consumer Affairs
500 James Robertson Parkway
Nashville, TN 37243-0600
615-741-4737
800-342-8385 (toll free in TN)

Texas
Consumer Protection Division
Office of Attorney General
P.O. Box 12548
Austin, TX 78711
512-463-2070

Consumer Protection Division
Office of Attorney General
714 Jackson Street, Suite 800
Dallas, TX 75202-4506
214-742-8944

Consumer Protection Division
Office of Attorney General
6090 Surety Drive, Room 113
El Paso, TX 79905
915-772-9476

Consumer Protection Division
Office of Attorney General
1019 Congress Street, Suite 1550
Houston, TX 77002-1702
713-223-5886

Consumer Protection Division
Office of Attorney General
1208 Fourteenth Street, Suite 900
Lubbock, TX 79401-3997
806-747-5238

Consumer Protection Division
Office of Attorney General

3201 North McColl Road, Suite B
McAllen, TX 78501
210-682-4547

Consumer Protection Division
Office of Attorney General
115 East Travis Street, Suite 925
San Antonio, TX 78205-1607
512-225-4191

Office of Public Insurance Counsel
333 Guadalope, Suite 3-120
Austin, TX 78701
512-322-4143

For Dallas:
Dallas Consumer Protection
   Division
Health and Human Services
   Department
320 East Jefferson Boulevard
Suite 312
Dallas, TX 75203
214-948-4400
214-670-5216

Utah
Division of Consumer Protection
Department of Commerce
160 East 3rd South
P.O. Box 45804
Salt Lake City, UT 84145-0804
801-530-6001
801-530-6601 (fax)

Vermont
Public Protection Division
Office of Attorney General
109 State Street

Montpelier, VT 05609-1001
802-828-3171

Consumer Assurance Section
Department of Agriculture, Food,
    and Market
120 State Street
Montpelier, VT 05620-2901
802-828-2436

Virgin Islands
Department of Licensing and
    Consumer Affairs
Property and Procurement Building
Subbase #1, Room 205
St. Thomas, VI 00802
809-774-3130

Virginia
Antitrust and Consumer Litigation
    Section
Office of Attorney General
Supreme Court Building
101 North Eighth Street
Richmond, VA 23219
804-786-2116
800-451-1525 (toll free in VA)

State Division of Consumer Affairs
Department of Agriculture and
    Consumer Services
Room 101, Washington Building
P.O. Box 1163
Richmond, VA 23209
804-786-2042

Washington
Consumer Protection Division
Office of the Attorney General

P.O. Box 40118
Olympia, WA 98504-0118
206-753-6210

Consumer and Business Fair
    Practices Division
Office of Attorney General
900 Fourth Avenue, Suite 2000
Seattle, WA 98164
206-464-6684
800-551-4636 (toll free in WA)

Consumer and Business Fair
    Practices Division
Office of Attorney General
West 1116 Riverside Avenue
Spokane, WA 99201
509-456-3123

Consumer and Business Fair
    Practices Division
Office of Attorney General
1019 Pacific Avenue, 3rd Floor
Tacoma, WA 98402-4411
206-593-2904

For Seattle:
Fraud Division
900 Fourth Avenue, #1002
Seattle, WA 98164
206-296-9010

Seattle Department of Licenses &
    Consumer Affairs
600 Fourth Avenue, #102
Seattle, WA 98104-1893
206-684-8484
or

Seattle Department of Licenses &
Consumer Affairs
805 S. Dearborn Street
Seattle, WA 98134
206-386-1298
or
Seattle Department of Licenses &
Consumer Affairs
600 Fourth Avenue, #102
Seattle, WA 98104-1893
206-684-8405

West Virginia

Consumer Protection Division
Office of Attorney General
812 Quarrier Street, 6th Floor
Charleston, WV 25301
304-558-8986
800-368-8808 (toll free in WV)

Division of Weights and
Measures
Department of Labor
570 MacCorkle Avenue
St. Albans, WV 25177
304-348-7890

Wisconsin

Division of Trade and Consumer
Protection
Department of Agriculture, Trade,
and Consumer Protection
801 West Badger Road
P.O. Box 8911
Madison, WI 53708
608-266-9836
800-422-7128 (toll free in WI)

Division of Trade and Consumer
Protection
Department of Agriculture, Trade,
and Consumer Protection
927 Loring Street
Altoona, WI 54720
715-839-3848
800-422-7128 (toll free in WI)

Regional Offices

Division of Trade and Consumer
Protection
Department of Agriculture, Trade,
and Consumer Protection
200 North Jefferson Street
Suite 146A
Green Bay, WI 54301
414-448-5111
800-422-7128 (toll free in WI)

Consumer Protection Regional
Office
Department of Agriculture, Trade,
and Consumer Protection
3333 N. Mayfair Road, Suite 114
Milwaukee, WI 53222-3288
414-266-1231

Office of Consumer Protection and
Citizen Advocacy
Department of Justice
P.O. Box 7856
Madison, WI 53707-7856
608-266-1852
800-362-8189 (toll free)

Office of Consumer Protection
Department of Justice

Milwaukee State Office Building
819 North Sixth Street, Room 520
Milwaukee, WI 53203-1678
414-227-4948
800-362-8189 (toll free)

Wyoming

State Office

Office of Attorney General
123 State Capitol Building
Cheyenne, WY 82002
307-777-7874

State Utility Commissions
If your problem is about telephone
service, electrical service, or any
other public utility matter, contact
your state utility commission:

Alabama Public Service
Commission
P.O. Box 991
Montgomery, AL 36101-0991
205-242-5207
800-392-8050 (toll free in AL)

Alaska Public Utilities Commission
1016 West Sixth Avenue, Suite 400
Anchorage, AK 99501
907-276-6222
907-276-0160 (fax)

Arizona Corporation Commission
1200 West Washington Street
Phoenix, AZ 85007
602-542-3935
602-255-2105 (TDD)
800-222-7000 (toll free in AZ)

Arkansas Public Service
Commission
P.O. Box 400
Little Rock, AR 72203-0400
501-682-1453
800-482-1164 (toll free in AR—
complaints)

California Public Utilities
    Commission
505 Van Ness Avenue, Room 5218
San Francisco, CA 94102
415-703-3703
415-703-2032 (TDD)
800-649-7570 (toll free in CA—
complaints)

Colorado Public Utilities
    Commission
1580 Logan Street
Logan Tower—Office Level 2
Denver, CO 80203
303-894-2021
800-888-0170 (toll free in CO)

Connecticut Department of Public
    Utility Control
1 Central Park Plaza
New Britain, CT 06051
203-827-1553
800-382-4586 (toll free in CT)

Delaware Public Service
    Commission
1560 South DuPont Highway
P.O. Box 457
Dover, DE 19903

302-739-4247
800-282-8574 (toll free in DE)

District of Columbia Public
    Service Commission
450 Fifth Street, N.W.
Suite 800
Washington, DC 20001
202-626-5110

Florida Public Service
    Commission
101 East Gaines Street
Tallahassee, FL 32399-0850
904-488-7238
800-342-3552 (toll free in FL)

Georgia Public Service
    Commission
244 Washington Street, S.W.
Atlanta, GA 30334
404-656-4512
800-282-5813 (toll free in GA)

Hawaii Public Utilities
    Commission
465 South King Street, Room 103
Honolulu, HI 96813
808-586-2020

Idaho Public Utilities Commission
State House
Boise, ID 83720
208-334-3912

Illinois Commerce Commission
527 East Capitol Avenue

P.O. Box 19280
Springfield, IL 62794-9280
217-782-7907
217-782-7434 (TDD)

Indiana Utility Regulatory
    Commission
E306 IGC South
Indianapolis, IN 46204
317-232-2701

Iowa Utilities Board
Lucas State Office Building
5th Floor
Des Moines, IA 50319
515-281-5979

Kansas Corporation
    Commission
1500 SW Arrowhead Road
Topeka, KS 66604-4027
913-271-3166
800-662-0027 (toll free in KS)

Kentucky Public Service
    Commission
730 Schenkel Lane
P.O. Box 615
Frankfort, KY 40602
502-564-3940

Louisiana Public Service
    Commissioner
P.O. Box 91154
Baton Rouge, LA 70821-9154
504-342-6687
800-256-2413 (toll free in LA)

Maine Public Utilities Commission
State House Station 18
Augusta, ME 04333
207-289-3831
800-452-4699 (toll free in ME)

Maryland Public Service
    Commission
231 East Baltimore Street
Baltimore, MD 21202
410-333-6000
800-492-0474 (toll free in MD)

Massachusetts Department of
    Public Utilities
100 Cambridge Street
12th Floor
Boston, MA 02202
617-727-3500

Michigan Public Service
    Commission
6545 Mercantile Way
P.O. Box 30221
Lansing, MI 48909
517-334-6445
800-292-9555 (toll free in MI)
800-443-8926 (toll free TDD in MI)

Minnesota Public Utilities
    Commission
121 Seventh Place East
Suite 350
St. Paul, MN 55101-2147
612-296-7124
612-297-1200 (TDD)
800-657-3782 (toll free in MN)

Mississippi Public Service
    Commission
P.O. Box 1174
Jackson, MS 39215
601-961-5400
Northern District
800-356-6428 (toll free in MS)
Central District
800-356-6430 (toll free in MS)
Southern District
800-356-6429 (toll free in MS)

Missouri Public Service
    Commission
P.O. Box 360
Jefferson City, MO 65102
314-751-3243
800-392-4211 (toll free in MO)

Montana Public Service
    Commission
2701 Prospect Avenue
P.O. Box 202601
Helena, MT 59620-2601
406-444-6199

Nebraska Public Service
    Commission
300 The Atrium
1200 "N" Street
Lincoln, NE 68508
or
P.O. Box 94927
Lincoln, NE 68509-4927
402-471-3101
800-526-0017 (toll free in NE)

Nevada Public Service Commission
4045 S. Spencer Street
Suite A-44
Las Vegas, NV 89119
702-486-6550

New Hampshire Public Utilities
    Commission
8 Old Suncook Road
Building No. 1
Concord, NH 03301
603-271-2431
800-852-3793 (toll free in NH)

New Jersey Board of Public
    Utilities
Two Gateway Center
Newark, NJ 07102
201-648-2027
201-648-7983 (TDD)
800-621-0241 (toll free in NJ)

New Mexico Public Utility
    Commission
Marian Hall
224 East Palace Avenue
Sante Fe, NM 87501-2013
505-827-6940

New York Public Service
    Commission
3 Empire State Plaza
Albany, NY 12223
518-474-5527
800-342-3377 (toll free in NY—
complaints)
800-342-3355 (toll free in NY—

emergency service cutoff,
7:30 A.M.–7:30 P.M. Monday–Friday)

North Carolina Utilities
    Commission
P.O. Box 29510
Raleigh, NC 27626-0510
919-733-4249
919-733-9277 (consumer services
and complaints)

North Dakota Public Service
    Commission
State Capitol Building
Bismarck, ND 58505-0480
701-224-2400

Ohio Public Utilities Commission
180 East Broad Street
Columbus, OH 43266-0573
614-466-3292
614-466-8180 (TDD)
800-686-7826 (toll free in OH—
consumer services)
800-686-1570 (toll free TDD in OH)

Oklahoma Corporation
    Commission
Jim Thorpe Office Building
2101 Lincoln Boulevard
Oklahoma City, OK 73105
405-521-2264
800-522-8154 (toll free in OK)

Oregon Public Utility Commission
550 Capitol Street NE
Salem, OR 97310-1380

503-378-6611
800-522-2404 (toll free in OR)

Pennsylvania Public Utility
    Commission
P.O. Box 3265
Harrisburg, PA 17120
717-787-4301
800-782-1110 (toll free in PA)

Puerto Rico Public Service
    Commission
Call Box 870
Hato Rey, PR 00919-0870
809-758-6264

Rhode Island Public Utilities
    Commission
100 Orange Street
Providence, RI 02903
401-277-3500 (voice/TDD)
800-341-1000 (toll free in RI)

South Carolina Public Service
    Commission
P.O. Drawer 11649
Columbia, SC 29211
803-737-5270
800-922-1531 (toll free in SC)

South Dakota Public Utilities
    Commission
500 East Capitol Avenue
Pierre, SD 57501-5070
605-773-3201
800-332-1782 (toll free in SD)

Tennessee Public Service
    Commission
460 James Robertson Parkway
Nashville, TN 37243-0505
615-741-3125
800-342-8359 (toll free voice/TDD
    in TN)

Texas Public Utility Commission
7800 Shoal Creek Boulevard
Suite 400N
Austin, TX 78757
512-458-0100
512-458-0221 (TDD)

Utah Public Service Commission
160 East 300 South
Salt Lake City, UT 84111
801-530-6716
801-530-6706 (TDD)

Vermont Public Service Board
89 Main Street, Drawer 20
Montpelier, VT 05620-2701
802-828-2358

Virgin Islands Public Services
    Commission
P.O. Box 40
Charlotte Amalie
St. Thomas, VI 00804
809-776-1291
809-774-4971 (fax)

Virginia State Corporation
    Commission
P.O. Box 1197

Richmond, VA 23209
804-371-9208
800-552-7945 (toll free in VA)

Washington Utilities and
   Transportation Commission
P.O. Box 47250
Olympia, WA 98504-7250
206-753-6423
800-562-6150 (toll free in WA)

West Virginia Public Service
   Commission
P.O. Box 812
Charleston, WV 25323
304-340-0300
800-344-5113 (toll free in WV)

Wisconsin Public Service
   Commission
4802 Sheboygan Avenue 53702
P.O. Box 7854
Madison, WI 53707-7854
608-266-2001
608-777-5700 (fax)

Wyoming Public Service
   Commission
700 West 21st Street
Cheyenne, WY 82002
307-777-7427

**Federal Agencies That Might
Assist You**

*To report violations of the telephone
order rule, contact:*

The Federal Trade Commission
Sixth and Pennsylvania Avenue,
N.W., Room 130
Washington, DC 20580
202-326-2222

*Consumer Information Center
(CIC)*
CIC publishes the free Consumer
Information Catalog, which lists
more than two hundred free and
low-cost federal booklets on a wide
variety of consumer topics. For a free
copy of the catalog, write to
Consumer Information Catalog,
Pueblo, CO 81009, or call 719-948-
4000.

Civil Rights Division
Look in your telephone directory
under "U.S. Government, Justice
Department, Civil Rights Division."
If it does not appear, call the appro-
priate FIC number or contact:

Civil Rights Division
Department of Justice
Washington, DC 20530
202-514-2151
202-514-0716 (TDD)

Airline Service Complaints
Office of Intergovernmental and
   Consumer Affairs (I-25)
Department of Transportation
Washington, DC 20590
202-366-2220

To report fraudulent import practices, call U.S. Customs Service's Fraud Hot Line:
800-ITS-FAKE (toll free)

Complaints about telephone systems:
Common Carrier Bureau
Informal Complaints Branch
Federal Communications
    Commission
2025 M Street, N.W., Room 6202
Washington, DC 20554
202-632-7553

Complaints about radio or television:
Mass Media Bureau
Complaints and Investigations
Federal Communications
    Commission
2025 M Street, N.W., Room 8210
Washington, DC 20554
202-632-7048

Complaints about cable programming rates:
Federal Communications
    Commission
Cable Form Request 329
P.O. Box 18238
Washington, DC 20036

Call the CPSC hotline to report a hazardous product or product-related injury between 10:00 A.M. and 3:00 P.M. weekdays. Recorded messages on safety recommendations and product recalls are available at all times. Call or write:

Product Safety Hotline
U.S. Consumer Product Safety
    Commission
Washington, DC 20207
800-638-CPSC (toll free)
800-638-2772 (toll free)
800-638-8270 (toll free TDD)

For mail fraud and other consumer problems in which mail service was involved, contact the Postal Crime Hot Line:
1-800-654-8896

For consumer education material or to file a complaint about consumer products other than cars, food, or drugs:
Product Safety Hotline
U.S. Consumer Product Safety
    Commission
Washington, DC 20207
800-638-CPSC (toll free)
800-492-8104 (toll free TDD in MD)
800-638-8270 (toll free TDD outside of MD)

To complain about safety of vehicles, child safety seats, and other motor vehicle equipment:
Auto Safety Hotline
National Highway Traffic Safety
    Administration
Department of Transportation
Washington, DC 20590
202-366-0123
202-366-7800 (TDD)

800-424-9393 (toll free outside DC)
800-424-9153 (toll free TDD outside DC)

Recalls
Item 595Z
Pueblo, CO 81009
(Write to this address to receive a free publication prepared by the U.S. Office of Consumer Affairs that explains which federal agencies issue consumer product recalls, the kinds of products each of them covers, how to report product safety problems, and how to find out about warnings or recalls that have been announced.)

National Consumer Organizations

Some of these can and will, in fact, help you with specific problems.

Alliance Against Fraud in Telemarketing (AAFT)
c/o National Consumers League
815 Fifteenth Street, N.W.
Suite 928-N
Washington, DC 20005
202-639-8140
202-347-0646 (fax)

Call for Action
3400 Idaho Avenue, N.W., Suite 101
Washington, DC 20016
202-537-0585
202-244-4881 (fax)

(Hot line for consumers with marketplace problems. Helps consumers through mediation of marketplace disputes.)

Consumer Action (CA)
116 New Montgomery, Suite 233
San Francisco, CA 94105
415-777-9635 (consumer complaint hot line, 10:00 A.M.–3:00 P.M., PST)
415-777-5267 (fax)
(Consumer Action does assist consumers with problems, especially in banking and telecommunications issues.)

National Fraud Information Center (NFIC)
c/o National Consumers League
815 Fifteenth Street, N.W.
Suite 928-N
Washington, DC 20005
800-876-7060 (toll free — TDD available)
202-347-0646 (fax)
(NFIC helps consumers file complaints about fraud, including referral to law enforcement agencies and professional associations.)

Consumer Affairs Divisions of Major Corporations

Consumer Affairs
AETNA Life and Casualty
151 Farmington Avenue

Hartford, CT 06156
203-273-0123
800-US-AETNA (toll free outside
CT)

Director of Consumer Affairs
    AT&T
295 North Maple Avenue
Room 2334F2
Basking Ridge, NJ 07920
908-221-5311

Customer Service
Ace Hardware Corporation
2200 Kensington Court
Oak Brook, IL 60521
708-990-6600

Admiral; see Maycor Appliance
Parts and Service Company

Customer Response Center
Alamo Rent A Car
P.O. Box 22776
Ft. Lauderdale, FL 33335
305-522-0000
800-327-0400 (toll free)

Consumer Affairs Department
Allied Van Lines
P.O. Box 4403
Chicago, IL 60680
708-717-3590

Customer Relations Manager
Allstate Insurance Company
Allstate Plaza—F4

Northbrook, IL 60062
708-402-6005

Consumer Services
Alpo Pet Foods
P.O. Box 25100
Lehigh Valley, PA 18003
800-366-6033 (toll free)

Vice President of Consumer
    Relations
Amana Refrigeration, Inc.
Amana, IA 52204
800-843-0304 (toll free—product
questions)

Customer Relations—Passenger
    Services
America West Airlines
4000 East Sky Harbor Boulevard
Phoenix, AZ 85034
800-235-9292

Manager, Consumer Relations
American Airlines, Inc.
P.O. Box 619612 MD 2400
DFW International Airport, TX
75261-9612
817-967-2000

Approved Auto Repair
American Automobile Association
Mailspace 15
1000 AAA Drive
Heathrow, FL 32746-5063
(written complaints only)

Executive Customer Relations
American Express Company
American Express Tower
World Financial Center
New York, NY 10285
212-640-4753
800-528-4800 (toll free—green card inquiries)
800-327-2177 (toll free—gold card inquiries)
800-525-3355 (toll free—platinum card inquiries)

Customer Relations and Consumer Affairs
Amoco Oil Company
200 East Randolph Drive
Chicago, IL 60601
800-333-3991 (toll free)

Director, Customer Relations
Amtrak
Washington Union Station
60 Massachusetts Avenue, N.E.
Washington, DC 20002
202-906-2121
800-USA-RAIL (toll free reservations and information)

Director, Distributor/Customer Services
Amway Corporation
7575 East Fulton Road
Ada, MI 49355
616-676-7717
800-548-3878 (toll free TDD)

Manager, Customer and Product Services
Andersen Windows, Inc.
100 Fourth Avenue North
Bayport, MN 55003
612-430-7255

Manager, Consumer Relations
Anheuser-Busch, Inc.
One Busch Place
St. Louis, MO 63118-1852
314-577-3093

Customer Relations Department
Apple Computer, Inc.
20525 Mariani Avenue
Cupertino, CA 95014
800-776-2333 (toll free—complaints and questions)
800-538-9696 (toll free—dealer information)

Aramis, Inc.; see Estée Lauder Companies

Consumer Communications
Armour Swift Eckrich
2001 Butterfield Road
Downers Grove, IL 60515
708-512-1000
800-325-7424 (toll free—Eckrich products)

Manager, Consumer Affairs
Armstrong Tire Division

Pirelli/Armstrong Tire
    Corporation
500 Sargent Drive
New Haven, CT 06536
800-243-0167 (toll free)

General Manager of U.S. Sales and
    Marketing
Atari Video Game Systems
1196 Borregas Avenue
Sunnyvale, CA 94089
408-745-2098

Manager, Customer Relations
Atlantic Richfield Company
ARCO Products Company
1055 W. Seventh Street
Los Angeles, CA 90051-0570
800-322-ARCO (toll free)

Customer Service
Atlas Van Lines
P.O. Box 509
Evansville, IN 47703-0509
800-252-8885 (toll free)

Supervisor, Customer Service
Avis Rent-A-Car System
900 Old Country Road
Garden City, NY 11530
516-222-4200

Consumer Information Center
Avon Products, Inc.
9 West Fifty-seventh Street
New York, NY 10019
212-546-6015

Bali Company
3330 Healy Drive
P.O. Box 5100
Winston-Salem, NC 27113
800-654-6122 (toll free — consumer
services)

Customer Relations #3538
Bank of America, NT & SA
Box 37000
San Francisco, CA 94137
415-241-7677

Eddie Bauer Customer Service
P.O. Box 3700
Seattle, WA 98124-3700
800-426-6253

Manager, Regulatory and
    Consumer Affairs
Contact Lens Care Products
OTC Health Care Products
Bausch and Lomb
Personal Products Division
1400 North Goodman Street
Rochester, NY 14692
800-553-5340 (toll free)

Director, Customer Service
Contact Lenses
Bausch and Lomb
Contact Lens Division
1400 North Goodman Street
Rochester, NY 14609
800-552-7388 (toll free)

Manager, Consumer Affairs
Eyewear Division

Bausch and Lomb
P.O. Box 478
Rochester, NY 14692-0478
800-343-5594 (toll free)

Customer Service
L.L. Bean, Inc.
Casco Street
Freeport, ME 04033-0001
800-341-4341 (toll free)
800-545-0090 (toll free TDD)

Director, Consumer Affairs
Best Foods
CPC International, Inc.
P.O. Box 8000 International Plaza
Englewood Cliffs, NJ 07632
201-994-2324

Manager, Customer Service
Best Western International
P.O. Box 42007
Phoenix, AZ 85080-2007
800-528-1238

Birds Eye; see General Foods
Corporation

Manager, Consumer Assistance
    and Information
Black and Decker Household
    Products
6 Armstrong Road
Shelton, CT 06484
800-231-9786

Consumer Services
Black and Decker Power Tools

626 Hanover Pike
Hampstead, MD 21074
410-239-5300
800-762-6672 (toll free)

Senior Vice President of
    Operations
Blockbuster Entertainment
    Corporation
One Blockbuster Plaza
Ft. Lauderdale, FL 33301
305-832-3000

Customer Service Department
Bloomingdale's by Mail, Ltd.
475 Knotter Drive
P.O. Box 593
Cheshire, CT 06410-9933
203-271-1313 (mail order inquiries
only)

Consumer Affairs
Blue Cross and Blue Shield
    Association
1310 G Street, N.W., 12th Floor
Washington, DC 20005
202-626-4780

Consumer Response Department
Borden, Inc.
180 East Broad Street
Columbus, OH 43215
614-225-4511

Manager, Consumer Affairs
Bradlees Discount Department
    Stores

One Bradlees Circle
P.O. Box 9015
Braintree, MA 02184-9015
617-380-5377

Consumer Affairs
Bridgestone/Firestone, Inc.
2550 W. Golf Road, Suite 400
Rolling Meadows, IL 60008
800-367-3872 (toll free)

Manager, Consumer Affairs
Bristol-Myers Products
685 Routes 202/206 North
Somerville, NJ 08876-1279
800-468-7746 (toll free)

Director, Public Affairs
Bristol-Myers Squibb
    Pharmaceutical Group
P.O. Box 4000
Princeton, NJ 08543-4000
609-252-4000
800-332-2056 (toll free)

Customer Relations
British Airways
75-20 Astoria Blvd.
Jackson Heights, NY 11370
718-397-4000

Customer Relations
Budget Rent A Car Corporation
P.O. Box 111580
Carrollton, TX 75011-1580
800-621-2844 (toll free)

President
Burlington Coat Factory
    Warehouse Corporation
1830 Route 130 North
Burlington, NJ 08016
609-387-7800

Manager, Professional Information
    Services
Burroughs Wellcome Company
3030 Cornwallis Road
Research Triangle Park, NC 27709
919-248-3000, ext. 4511

Consumer Affairs Department
CIBA Consumer Pharmaceuticals
581 Main Street
Woodbridge, NJ 07095
908-602-6780

Ciba-Geigy Corporation
Plant Protection
410 Swing Road
Greensboro, NC 27409
919-632-6000
800-334-9481 (toll free)

Ciba-Geigy Corporation
Pharmaceuticals Division
556 Morris Avenue
Summit, NJ 07901-1398
908-277-5000

CIBA Vision Corporation
11460 John Creek Parkway
Duluth, GA 30136
800-227-1524, ext. 4435 (toll free —
consumer relations)

Customer Service
CIE America
2515 McCave Way
P.O. Box 19663
Irvine, CA 92713-9663
800-877-1421, ext. 4260 (toll free)

Customer Relations Department
CVS
One CVS Drive
Woonsocket, RI 02895-0988
401-765-1500
800-444-1140 (toll free)

Caloric Modern Maid
Corporation; see Amana
Refrigeration, Inc.

Manager, Consumer Center
Campbell Soup Company
Campbell Place
Camden, NJ 08103-1799
609-342-3714

Customer Relations Department
Canon U.S.A., Inc.
One Canon Plaza
Lake Success, NY 11042
516-328-4215

Guest Relations Manager
Carnival Cruise Lines
3655 Northwest Eighty-seventh
    Avenue
Miami, FL 33178-2428
800-327-7373 (toll free)

Customer Relations Manager
Carrier Air Conditioning
    Company
P.O. Box 4808
Syracuse, NY 13221
800-227-7437 (toll free)
Bryant Heating and Air
Conditioning
800-428-4326 (toll free)
Day & Night Heating and Air
Conditioning
800-428-4326 (toll free)
Payne Heating and Air
Conditioning
800-428-4326 (toll free)

Carte Blanche; see Diners Club

Customer Service Department
Casio, Inc.
570 Mount Pleasant Avenue
Dover, NJ 07801
201-361-5400

Consumer Relations
Chanel, Inc.
9 West Fifty-seventh Street
44th Floor
New York, NY 10019
212-688-5055

Director, Consumer
    Information
Cheesebrough-Pond's, USA
55 Merritt Boulevard
Trumbull, CT 06611
800-243-5804

Dealer and Consumer Affairs
Chevron U.S.A. Inc.
P.O. Box H
Concord, CA 94524
800-962-1223 (toll free)

Guest Relations
Chi-Chi's, Inc.
10200 Linn Station Road
Louisville, KY 40223
502-426-3900

Circuit City Stores, Inc.
9950 Mayland Drive
Richmond, VA 23233
804-527-4000
800-251-2665 (toll free)

Corporate Director of Customer
    Affairs
Citicorp/Citibank
399 Park Avenue
New York, NY 10043
212-559-0043

Consumer Affairs Dept.
Clairol, Inc.
300 Park Avenue South
New York, NY 10010
800-223-5800 (toll free voice/TDD)
800-HISPANA (toll free Spanish
voice/TDD)

Clinique Laboratories, Inc.; see
Estée Lauder Companies

Consumer Services Manager
Clorox Company

1221 Broadway
Oakland, CA 94612-1888
510-271-7283
800-292-2200 (toll free — laundry
brands)
800-537-2823 (toll free — charcoal
and food brands)
800-227-1860 (toll free — household
surface cleaners)
800-426-6228 (toll free — insecticides)
800-242-7482 (toll free — water
purification systems)

Consumer Affairs Department
Club Med Sales, Inc.
40 West Fifty-seventh Street
New York, NY 10019
212-977-2100

Industry and Consumer Affairs
The Coca-Cola Company
P.O. Drawer 1734
Atlanta, GA 30301
800-438-2653 (toll free)
800-262-2653 (toll free TDD)

Corporate Office
Coldwell Banker Corp.
27271 Los Rambals
Mission Viejo, CA 92629
714-367-1800

Associate Director, Consumer
    Response
U.S. Consumer Affairs
Colgate-Palmolive Company
300 Park Avenue

New York, NY 10022-7499
800-221-4607 (toll free—oral care products)
800-338-8388 (toll free—household products)

Customer Relations Department
Compaq Computer Corporation
P.O. Box 692000
Houston, TX 77269-2000
800-345-1518 (toll free)

Director of Warranty
    Administration and Control
Congoleum Corporation
Technical Operations Center
861 Sloan Avenue
Trenton, NJ 08619
609-584-3000
800-274-3266 (toll free)

Director, Customer Relations
Continental Airlines, Inc.
3663 North Belt East, Suite 500
Houston, TX 77032
713-987-6500

Coors Brewing Company
Corporate Communications
    Manager
Consumer Information Center
NH320
Golden, CO 80401
800-642-6116 (toll free)

Coppertone; see Schering-Plough
HealthCare Products, Inc.

Corning/Revere Consumer
    Information Center
Corning Incorporated
1300 Hopeman Parkway
Waynesboro, VA 22980
800-999-3436

Consumer Affairs Division
Jenny Craig International
445 Marine View Avenue
Del Mar, CA 92014
619-259-7000

Director, Sales and Marketing
    Operations
Cuisinarts Corporation
P.O. Box 120067
Stamford, CT 06912
203-975-4600
609-426-1300 (in NJ)
800-726-0190 (toll free outside NJ)

Dairy Queen; see International
Dairy Queen

Director, Consumer Relations
Dannon Company, Inc.
1111 Westchester Avenue
White Plains, NY 10604
(written inquiries only)

Consumer Division
Danskin
P.O. Box 15016
York, PA 17405-7016
800-288-6749

Central Consumer Relations
Dayton's, Hudson's, Marshall
   Field's Department Stores
Box 875
700 Nicollet Mall
Minneapolis, MN 55402
612-375-3382

Director, Consumer Affairs
Del Monte Foods
P.O. Box 193575
San Francisco, CA 94119-3575
800-543-3090 (toll free)

Director, Consumer Affairs
Delta Air Lines
Hartsfield Atlanta International
   Airport
Atlanta, GA 30320
404-715-1402

Product Service Manager
Delta Faucets
P.O. Box 40980
Indianapolis, IN 46280
317-848-1812

Operations
Denny's, Inc.
203 East Main St.
Spartanburg, SC 29319-0001
803-596-8000

Customer Relations Department
Digital Equipment Corporation
40 Old Bolton Road

Stow, MA 01775-1215
508-493-7161
800-332-4636 (toll free)

Customer Relations
Dillard Department Stores, Inc.
1600 Cantrell Road
Little Rock, AR 72202
501-376-5200

Vice President, Customer Service
Diners Club International
183 Inverness Drive West
Englewood, CO 80112
303-799-9000
800-234-6377 (toll free)
303-643-2155 (TDD)

Manager, Consumer Response
Dole Packaged Foods
ATTN: Consumer Response
   Department
5795 Lindero Canyon Road
Westlake Village, CA 91362-4013
800-232-8888 (toll free)

President
Domino's Pizza, Inc.
P.O. Box 997
Ann Arbor, MI 48106-0997
313-930-3030

Manager, Consumer Affairs
DowBrands
P.O. Box 68511
Indianapolis, IN 46268-0511
800-428-4795 (toll tree)

Coordinator, Consumer Affairs
Dr Pepper/Seven-Up Companies, Inc.
(Welch's & IBC Root Beer)
P.O. Box 655086
Dallas, TX 75265-5086
214-360-7000

Chairman of the Board
Dunkin Donuts of America
P.O. Box 317
Randolph, MA 02368
617-961-4000

Manager, Consumer Affairs and OE Service
Dunlop Tire Corporation
P.O. Box 1109
Buffalo, NY 14240-1109
800-548-4714 (toll free)

Customer Information Center
DuPont Company
BMP/Reeves Mill
Wilmington, DE 19880-0010
800-441-7515 (toll free)

Consumer Affairs Department
Duracell USA
Division of Duracell, Inc.
Berkshire Corporate Park
Bethel, CT 06801
203-796-4300
800-551-2355 (toll free 8:30 A.M.–5:00 P.M. EST)

Eastman Kodak Company
343 State Street

Rochester, NY 14650-0811
800-242-2424 (toll free)

Customer Service Representative
Eckerd Drug Company
8333 Bryan Dairy Road
P.O. Box 4689
Clearwater, FL 34618
813-399-6000

Electrolux Corporation
2300 Windy Ridge Parkway
Suite 900
Marietta, GA 30067
404-933-1000
800-243-9078 (toll free)

Retail Customer Service Department
Esprit Corp.
900 Minnesota Street
San Francisco, CA 94107-3000
415-648-6900
800-777-8765 (toll free)

Vice President, Consumer Relations
Estée Lauder Companies
767 Fifth Avenue
New York, NY 10153-0003
212-572-4200

Supervisor, Consumer Affairs
Ethan Allen, Inc.
Ethan Allen Drive
Danbury, CT 06811
203-743-8553

Consumer Relations Manager
The Eureka Company
1201 East Bell Street
Bloomington, IL 61701-6902
309-823-5735
800-282-2886 (toll free — warranty
center)

Mr. Dan Evans, Chairman of the
    Board
Bob Evans Farms, Inc.
3776 South High Street
P.O. Box 07863
Columbus, OH 43207
614-491-2225
800-272-PORK (toll free outside OH)

Consumer Affairs Team Leader
Exxon Company U.S.A.
P.O. Box 2180
Houston, TX 77252-2180
713-656-2111

Manager, Corporate Quality
Federal Express Corporation
P.O Box 727, Department 2142
Memphis, TN 38194-2142
901-395-4539
800-238-5355 (toll free)

Director, Community Relations
    and Operations
Federated Department Stores
7 West Seventh Street
Cincinnati, OH 45202
513-579-7000

Manager, Consumer Affairs
Fisher Price
636 Girard Avenue
East Aurora, NY 14052-1880
800-432-5437 (toll free)

Florsheim Shoe Company
130 South Canal Street
Chicago, IL 60606-3999
312-559-2500

Manager, Consumer Affairs
The Frigidaire Co.
6000 Perimeter Drive
Dublin, OH 43017
800-374-7714
800-451-7007 (toll free — Frigidaire
Appliances)
800-485-1445 (toll free — Gibson
Appliances)
800-323-7773 (toll free — Kelvinator
Appliance Company)
800-537-5530 (toll free — O'Keefe &
Merit Appliances)
800-537-5530 (toll tree — Tappan
Company, Inc.)
800-245-0600 (toll free — White
Westinghouse)

Director, Consumer Services
Fruit of the Loom, Inc.
One Fruit of the Loom Drive
Bowling Green, KY 42102-9015
502-781-6400

Customer Service Department
Fuji Photo Film U.S.A., Inc.

400 Commerce Boulevard
Carlstadt, NJ 07072-3009
800-659-3854, ext. 2571 (toll free)

Manager, Consumer Relations
Ernest & Julio Gallo Winery
P.O. Box 1130
Modesto, CA 95353
209-579-3161

General Electric Company
For information on GE consumer
products and services, call:
GE answer center service
800-626-2000 (toll free)

Manager of Consumer Response
    and Information Center
General Foods Corporation
250 North Street
White Plains, NY 10625
800-431-1001 (toll free — General
Foods products)

Assistant Manager, Consumer
    Services
General Mills, Inc.
P.O. Box 1113
Minneapolis, MN 55440-1113
612-540-4295
800-328-6787 (toll free — bakery
products)
800-328-1144 (toll free — cereals)
800-222-6846 (toll free — Gorton's)
800-231-0308 (toll free — snacks)

Customer Relations Department
General Motors Acceptance
    Corporation (GMAC)
3044 West Grand Boulevard
Room AX348
Detroit, MI 48202
313-556-0510
800-441-9234 (toll free)
800-TDD-GMAC (toll tree TDD)

Georgia-Pacific Corp.
P.O. Box 105605
Atlanta, GA 30348-5605
404-220-6227 (building products)
404-527-0038 (paper products)

Director, Corporate
    Communications
Gerber Products Company
445 State Street
Fremont, MI 49413-1056
616-928-2000
800-4-GERBER (toll free — twenty-
four hours)
800-421-4221 (toll free — twenty-four-
hour breast-feeding advice)
800-828-9119 (toll free — baby
formula)

Vice President for Consumer
    Affairs
Giant Food Inc.
P.O. Box 1804, Department 597
Washington, DC 20013
301-341-4365
301-341-4327 (TDD)

Manager, Consumer Affairs
Gillette Company
P.O. Box 61
Boston, MA 02199
617-463-3337

Director, Consumer Relations
Goodyear Tire & Rubber Co.
1144 East Market Street
Akron, OH 44316
216-796-4940
216-796-6055 (TDD)
800-321-2136 (toll free)

Manager, Customer Relations
Greyhound Lines, Inc.
P.O. Box 660362
Dallas, TX 75266-0362
214-419-3914

Guess? Inc.
1444 South Alameda Street
Los Angeles, CA 90021
213-765-3100

Consumer Relations Department
Hartz Mountain Corporation
700 Frank E. Rodgers Boulevard
    South
Harrison, NJ 07029-9987
201-481-4800

Supervisor, Consumer Affairs
Hasbro, Inc.
P.O. Box 200
Pawtucket, RI 02861-0200
800-255-5516

Manager, Consumer Affairs
Heinz U.S.A.
P.O. Box 57
Pittsburgh, PA 15230-0057
412-237-5740

Consumer Affairs Department
Consumer Brands
Helene Curtis, Inc.
325 North Wells Street
Chicago, IL 60610-4713
312-661-0222

Manager, Consumer Relations
Hershey Foods Corporation
P.O. Box 815
Hershey, PA 17033-0815
800-468-1714 (toll free)

Manager, Executive Customer
    Relations
Hertz Corporation
225 Brae Boulevard
Park Ridge, NJ 07656-0713
201-307-2000
800-654-3131 (toll free —
reservations)
800-654-2280 (toll free
TDD)

Customer Information Center
Hewlett-Packard Company
19310 Prune Ridge Avenue
Cupertino, CA 95014
408-246-4300

Hilton Hotels Corporation
9336 Civic Center Drive

Beverly Hills, CA 90209-5567
310-278-4321

Hitachi Home Electronics
    (America), Inc.
3890 Steve Reynolds Boulevard
Norcross, GA 30093
404-279-5600
800-241-6558 (toll free)

Mr. Randall Smith
Holiday Inn Worldwide
Three Ravinia Drive, Suite 2000
Atlanta, GA 30346
404-604-2000

Director, Consumer Affairs
Home Depot Inc.
2727 Paces Ferry Road
Atlanta, GA 30339
404-433-8211

Manager, Consumer Affairs
Residential Division
Honeywell, Inc.
Honeywell Plaza
P.O. Box 524
Minneapolis, MN 55440-0524
612-951-1000
800-468-1502 (toll free)

Manager of Consumer Response
    Center
Hoover Company
101 East Maple
North Canton, OH 44720
800-944-9200 (toll free)

Director, Consumer Affairs
Hormel Foods Company
501 Sixteenth Avenue, N.E.
Austin, MN 55912-9989
507-437-5395

Hunt-Wesson, Inc.
P.O. Box 4800
Fullerton, CA 92634-4800
714-680-1431

Director, Quality Assurance
Hyatt Hotels & Resorts
200 West Madison Street
39th Floor
Chicago, IL 60606
312-750-1234
800-228-3336 (toll free)

IBM Information Support Center
300 East Valencia
Tucson, AZ 85706
800-426-3333

Communications Department
International Dairy Queen, Inc.
P.O. Box 39286
7505 Metro Boulevard
Minneapolis, MN 55439-0286
612-830-0200

Jenn-Air Company; see Maycor
Appliance Parts and Service
Company

Consumer Relations
Jockey International, Inc.

2300 Sixtieth Street
Kenosha, WI 53140
414-658-8111

Johnson & Johnson Consumer
    Products, Inc.
Information Center
199 Grandview Road
Skillman, NJ 08558
800-526-3967 (toll free)

Manager, Guest Services
Howard Johnson, Inc.
P.O. Box 29004
Phoenix, AZ 85038
602-389-5555

Manager, Customer Service
Kmart Corporation
3100 West Big Beaver Road
Troy, MI 48084
800-63-KMART (toll free)

Consumer Services
Kawasaki Motor Corporation,
    U.S.A.
P.O. Box 25252
Santa Ana, CA 92799-5252
714-770-0400

Consumer Communications
Keebler Company, Inc.
One Hollow Tree Lane
Elmhurst, IL 60126
708-833-2900

Director, Consumer Affairs
Kellogg Company
P.O. Box CAMB
Battle Creek, MI 49016
800-962-1413

Manager, Product Service
The Kelly Springfield Tire
    Company
12501 Willow Brook Road, S.E.
Cumberland, MD 21502-2599
301-777-6635
301-777-6017

Kelvinator Appliance Company;
see The Frigidaire Co.

Director, Consumer Services
Kimberly-Clark Corporation
P.O. Box 2020
Neenah, WI 54957-2020
414-721-8000
800-544-1847 (toll free)

Consumer Assistance Center
KitchenAid
701 Main Street
St. Joseph, MO 49085-1392
616-923-4500
800-422-1230 (toll free)

Assistant to the Senior Vice
    President
Public Relations and
    Communications
Calvin Klein Industries, Inc.
205 West Thirty-ninth Street

10th Floor
New York, NY 10018
212-719-2600
800-327-8731 (toll free)

Service and Technical Publications
Kohler Company
Kohler, WI 53044
414-457-4441

Manager, Consumer Affairs
Plumbing and Specialty Products
Kohler Company
Kohler, WI 53044
414-457-4441

ATTN: Consumer Response
    Center
Kraft, Inc.
Kraft Court
Glenview, IL 60025
800-323-0768 (toll free)

Customer Relations Manager
Kroger Company
1014 Vine Street
Cincinnati, OH 45201
513-762-1589
800-632-6900 (toll free — product
information)

Manager of Consumer Services
La-Z-Boy Chair Company
1284 North Telegraph Road
Monroe, MI 48161-3309
313-242-1444

Manager, Consumer Affairs
Land O'Lakes, Inc.
P.O. Box 116
Minneapolis, MN 55440-0116
800-328-4155 (toll free)

Customer Service
Land's End
One Land's End Lane
Dodgeville, WI 53595
800-356-4444 (toll free)

Vice President, Retail Service
Lechmere
275 Wildwood Street
Woburn, MA 01801
617-476-1404
800-733-4666 (toll free)

L'eggs Products
Sara Lee Hosiery
Sara Lee Corporation
5660 University Parkway
Winston-Salem, NC 27105
919-519-2529

Lennox Industries
P.O Box 799900
Dallas, TX 75379-9900
214-497-5000

Consumer and Public Relations
    Department
Lever Brothers Company
390 Park Avenue
New York, NY 10022-4698
800-598-1223 (toll free)

Consumer Affairs
Levi Strauss & Co.
1155 Battery Street
San Francisco, CA 94111
800-USA-LEVI (toll free)

Vice President, Consumer
    Relations
Levitz Furniture Corporation
6111 Broken Sound Parkway, N.W.
Boca Raton, FL 33487-2799
800-631-4601 (toll free)

Customer Service
Levolor Corporation
7614 Business Park Drive
Greensboro, NC 27409
800-LEVOLOR (toll free)

Customer Service
Lillian Vernon Corporation
2600 International Parkway
Virginia Beach, VA 23452
804-430-1500

Consumer Communications
Eli Lilly & Company
Lilly Corporate Center
Indianapolis, IN 46285
317-276-8588
(For medical information, contact
your physician.)

Vice President
Financial and Public Relations
The Limited, Inc.
Two Limited Parkway

P.O. Box 16000
Columbus, OH 43216
614-479-7000

Manager
Customer Service Center
Little Caeser Enterprises
2211 Woodward Avenue
Detroit, MI 48201
800-7-CAESAR

Customer Relations Manager
Lorillard Tobacco Company
2525 East Market Street
P.O. Box 21688
Greensboro, NC 27420-1688
919-373-6669

Senior Vice President
Consumer Service
MCI Consumer Markets
1200 South Hayes Street, 12th Floor
Arlington, VA 22202
703-415-3195

Consumer Affairs Department
M&M/Mars, Inc.
High Street
Hacketstown, NJ 07840
201-852-1000

Vice President
Customer Service
R.H. Macy & Company, Inc.
151 West Thirty-fourth Street
New York, NY 10001
212-695-4400

Magic Chef; see Maycor Appliance Parts and Service Company

Consumer Affairs
Marriott Corporation
One Marriott Drive
Attn: Department 921.60
Washington, DC 20058
301-380-7600

MasterCard International (contact issuing bank)
800-826-2181 (toll free—lost or stolen cards or questions about the MasterCard system)

Director, Consumer Affairs
Mattel Toys, Inc.
333 Continental Boulevard
El Segundo, CA 90245-5012
213-524-2000
800-524-TOYS

Max Factor; see Procter & Gamble Company

Maxwell House; see General Foods Corporation

Manager, Consumer Relations
Maybelline Inc.
P.O. Box 372
Memphis, TN 38101-0372
901-320-2166

Maycor Appliance Parts and
  Service Company

240 Edwards Street, S.E.
Cleveland, TN 37311
615-472-3333

McCrory Stores, Inc.
2955 East Market Street
York, PA 17402
717-757-8181

Manager, Customer Satisfaction
  Department
McDonald's Corporation
Kroc Drive
Oak Brook, IL 60521
708-575-6198

Customer Service Representative
Meineke Discount Muffler
128 South Tryon Street, Suite 900
Charlotte, NC 28202
704-377-3070

Associate Director, Consumer
  Affairs
Mennen Company
300 Park Avenue
New York, NY 10022
800-228-7408

Consumer Affairs Analyst
Mervyn's
25001 Industrial Boulevard
Hayward, CA 94545
415-786-8337

Consumer Relations Department
Michelin Tire Corporation

One Parkway South
Greenville, SC 29615
800-847-3435

Manager, Consumer Relations
Midas International Corporation
225 North Michigan Avenue
Chicago, IL 60601
800-621-8545

Consumer Service Coordinator
Milton Bradley Company
443 Shaker Road
East Long Meadow, MA 01028
413-525-6411

National Manager of Consumer
    Service
Minolta Corporation
100 Williams Drive
Ramsey, NJ 07446
201-825-4000

Consumer Relations
Mitsubishi Electronics America,
    Inc.
5665 Plaza Drive
P.O. Box 6007
Cypress, CA 90630-0007
714-220-1464

Manager, Quality and Customer
    Support
Mobil Oil Corporation
3225 Gallows Road
Fairfax, VA 22037
703-849-3994

Customer Services Manager
Mobil Oil Credit Corporation
11300 Corporate Avenue
Lenexa, KS 66219-1385
913-752-7000

Customer Relations Manager
Montgomery Ward
One Montgomery Ward Plaza, 9-S
Chicago, IL 60671
312-467-2000

Director of Marketing
Motorola, Inc.
1303 East Algonquin Road
Schaumburg, IL 60196
708-576-5000

Customer Service Manager
NEC Technologies Inc.
1255 Michael Drive
Wood Dale, IL 60191-1094
708-860-9500, ext. 4440

Manager, Consumer Information
    Services
Nabisco Foods Group
100 DeForest Ave.
East Hanover, NJ 07936
201-503-2617
800-NABISCO (toll free)

Manager, Consumer Affairs
National Car Rental System, Inc.
7700 France Avenue South
Minneapolis, MN 55435
612-830-2033
800-367-6767 (toll free)

Customer Service Department
Neiman-Marcus
P.O. Box 64780
Dallas, TX 75206
214-741-6911
800-442-2274 (toll free in TX)
800-527-1767 (toll free outside TX)

Director, Office of Consumer
 Affairs
Nestlé USA
800 North Brand Boulevard
Glendale, CA 91203
818-549-6579

Consumer Affairs
Neutrogena Corporation
5760 West Ninety-sixth Street
Los Angeles, CA 90045
310-642-1150
800-421-6857 (toll free outside CA)

Customer Service
Nexxus Products
P.O. Box 1274
Santa Barbara, CA 93116-9976
805-968-6900

Consumer Services
Nike, Inc.
Nike/World Campus
1 Bowerman Drive
Beaverton, OR 97005
503-671-6453
800-344-6453 (toll free outside OR)

Consumer Services
Nintendo of America Inc.

4820 150th Avenue NE
Redmond, WA 98052
800-255-3700 (toll free)

Department of Consumer
 Relations
Norelco Consumer Products
 Company
High Ridge Park
P.O. Box 10166
Stamford, CT 06904
800-243-7884

Norge; see Maycor Appliance Parts
and Service Company

Customer Relations
Northwest Airlines
C5270
5101 Northwest Drive
St. Paul, MN 55111-3034
612-726-2046
800-328-2298 (toll free TDD—
reservations)

Manager, Customer Service
Norwegian Cruise Line
95 Merrick Way
Miami, FL 33134
305-460-2796

The NutraSweet Company
1751 Lake Cook Road
Deerfield, IL 60015
800-321-7254 (toll free—
NutraSweet)
800-323-5316 (toll free—Equal)

Nutri/System Inc.
410 Horsham Road
Horsham, PA 10944
215-445-5300

Manager, Consumer Affairs
Ocean Spray Cranberries Inc.
One Ocean Spray Drive
Lakeville/Middleboro, MA 02349
508-946-7407

Manager, Customer Support
Olympus America
145 Crossways Park
Woodbury, NY 11797
516-364-3000

Manager, Consumer Services
Ortho Consumer Products
Chevron Chemical Company
P.O. Box 5047
San Ramon, CA 94583-0947
415-842-5539

Manager, Customer Service
Pella Corporation
102 Main Street
Pella, IA 50219
515-628-1000

Consumer Relations Manager
JCPenney Company, Inc.
P.O. Box 10001
Dallas, TX 75301-8222
214-431-8500

National Technical Service
   Manager

Pennzoil Products Company
P.O. Box 2967
Houston, TX 77252-2967
713-546-8783 (collect calls
accepted)

Peoples Drug Stores, Inc.; see CVS

Manager, Consumer Affairs
Pepperidge Farm, Inc.
595 Westport Avenue
Norwalk, CT 06851
203-846-7276

Manager, Public Affairs
Pepsi-Cola Company
1 Pepsi Way
Somers, NY 10589-2201
914-767-6000

Manager of Consumer Relations
Perdue Farms
P.O. Box 1537
Salisbury, MD 21802
410-543-3000
800-442-2034 (toll free outside MD)

Administrator of Consumer Affairs
Philip Morris Companies
   Incorporated
120 Park Avenue
New York, NY 10017
212-880-3366

Pillsbury Company
Consumer Response
P.O. Box 550

Minneapolis, MN 55440
800-767-4466 (toll free)

Division Manager, Customer
    Service
Pioneer Electronics Service, Inc.
P.O. Box 1760
Long Beach, CA 90810
800-421-1404 (toll free)

Supervisor, Consumer Affairs
Playskool
Consumer Affairs Dept.
P.O. Box 200
Pawtucket, RI 02862-0200
800-752-9755

Manager, Consumer Affairs
Playtex Apparel, Inc.
P.O. Box 631
MS 1526
Dover, DE 19903-0631
302-674-6000
800-537-9955 (toll free)

Playtex Family Products Corp.
215 College Road
P.O. Box 728
Paramus, NJ 07652
800-624-0825 (toll free in NJ)
800-222-0453 (toll free outside
NJ)

Customer Service Department
Polaroid Corporation
784 Memorial Drive
Cambridge, MA 02139

617-577-2000 (collect calls accepted
within MA)
800-343-5000 (toll free outside MA)

Consumer Relations Manager
Polo/Ralph Lauren Corporation
4100 Beechwood Drive
Greensboro, NC 27410
800-775-7656 (toll free)

Prescriptives, Inc.; see Estée
Lauder Companies

Manager, Consumer Services
Cosmetic and Fragrance Division
Procter & Gamble Company
11050 York Road
Hunt Valley, MD 21030-2098
410-785-4411
800-426-8374 (toll free)

Associate Director, Consumer
    Relations
Procter & Gamble Company
P.O. Box 599
Cincinnati, OH 45201-0599
513-945-8787
(Toll free numbers appear on all
Procter & Gamble product
labels.)

Director of Customer Relations
Publix Super Markets
1936 George Jenkins Boulevard
P.O. Box 407
Lakeland, FL 33802
813-688-1188

Director of Consumer Response
Quaker Oats Company
P.O. Box 049003
Chicago, IL 60604-9003
312-222-7843

Manager, Public Relations
Quaker State Corporation
P.O. Box 989
Oil City, PA 16301
814-676-7676

Radio Shack; see Tandy
Corporation/Radio Shack

Director, Office of Consumer
  Affairs
Ralston Purina Company
Checkerboard Square
St. Louis, MO 63164
314-982-4566
800-345-5678 (toll free)

Director, Corporate
  Communications
Ramada International Hotels and
  Resorts
2655 Lejeune Road, Suite 400
Coral Gables, FL 33134
305-460-1900

Orville Redenbacher; see Hunt-
Wesson, Inc.

Consumer Relations
Reebok International, Ltd.
100 Technology Center Drive

Stoughton, MA 02072
800-843-4444 (toll free)

Customer Service Manager
The Regina Company
P.O. Box 638
Long Beach, MS 39560
800-847-8336 (toll free)

Customer Relations Department
Remington Products Company
60 Main Street
Bridgeport, CT 06004
203-367-4400

Director, Revlon Consumer
  Information Center
P.O. Box 6113
Oxford, NC 27565
919-603-2828

Service Manager
Rolex Watch U.S.A. Inc.
665 Fifth Avenue
New York, NY 10022
212-758-7700

Director, Passenger Services–
  Customer Relations
Royal Viking Line
95 Merrick Way
Coral Gables, FL 33134
800-422-8000

Supervisor, Consumer Services
Rubbermaid, Inc.
1147 Akron Road

Wooster, OH 44691-0800
216-264-6464

Group Manager, Customer Service
Ryder Truck Rental
P.O. Box 020816
Miami, FL 33102-0816
800-327-7777 (toll free)

Public Affairs Department
    Manager
Safeway Inc.
Oakland, CA 94660
510-891-3267

Department Manager of Corporate
    Customer Service
Saks & Companies NY
12 East Forty-ninth Street
New York, NY 10022
212-940-5027
800-239-3089 (toll free)

Sara Lee Corporation
Three First National Plaza
70 West Madison Street
Chicago, IL 60602-4260
312-726-2600

Manager, Consumer Relations
Schering-Plough HealthCare
    Products, Inc.
3030 Jackson Avenue
Memphis, TN 38151-0001
901-320-2998

Scholl; see Schering-Plough
HealthCare Products, Inc.

Consumer Relations Department
Schwinn Bicycle Company
217 North Jefferson Street
Chicago, IL 60661-1111
800-633-0231 (toll free)

Manager, Consumer Relations
Scott Paper Company
Scott Plaza Two
Philadelphia, PA 19113
215-522-6760
800-835-7268 (toll free)

Consumer Relations
Joseph E. Seagram & Sons, Inc.
800 Third Avenue
New York, NY 10022
212-572-7335

Customer Service Representative
Sealy Mattress Manufacturing
    Company
1228 Euclid Avenue, 10th Floor
Cleveland, OH 44115
216-522-1310
216-522-1366 (TDD)

Customer Affairs Director
Seamans Furniture Company, Inc.
300 Crossways Park Dr.
Woodbury, NY 11797
516-682-1563
800-445-2503 (toll free)

Customer Service
G.D. Searle and Company
    Pharmaceuticals

P.O. Box 5110
Chicago, IL 60680
800-323-1603 (toll free)

National Customer Relations
    Manager
Sears Merchandise Group
3333 Beverly Road—731CR
Hoffman Estates, IL 60179
708-286-5188

Coserv
Seiko Corporation of America
27 McKee Drive
Mahwah, NJ 07430
201-529-3311

Customer Service
Serta, Inc.
2800 River Road
Des Plaines, IL 60018
708-699-9300
800-426-0371 (toll free)

Customer Relations
Sharp Electronics Corporation
Sharp Plaza
P.O. Box 650
Mahwah, NJ 07430-2135
201-529-8200
800-526-0264 (toll free)

Customer Relations
The Sharper Image
650 Davis Street
San Francisco, CA 94111
800-344-5555 (toll free)

Manager, Credit Card Marketing
    Programs
Shell Oil Company
Box 4650
Houston, TX 77252
800-248-4257

Product Information Department
Sherwin-Williams Company, Paint
    Stores Group
101 Prospect Avenue, N.W.
Cleveland, OH 44115-1075
216-566-2151

Consumer Affairs Department
Sewing Products Division
Singer Sewing Company
P.O. Box 1909
Edison, NJ 08818-1909
908-287-0707
800-877-7762

Consumer Services Department
SlimFast Foods Company
919 Third Avenue
New York, NY 10022-3898
800-862-4500 (toll free)

Consumer/Public Affairs
    Department
SmithKline Beecham Consumer
    Brands
P.O. Box 1467
Pittsburgh, PA 15230-1467
412-928-1000
800-245-1040 (toll free)

Manager of Communications
J.M. Smucker Company
Strawberry Lane
Orrville, OH 44667-0280
216-682-3000

Manager, National Customer
    Relations
Sony Corporation of America
Sony Service Company
One Sony Drive
Park Ridge, NJ 07656
800-282-2848

Director, Customer Relations
Southwest Airlines
Love Field
P.O. Box 36611
Dallas, TX 75235-1611
214-904-4223
800-533-1305 (toll free TDD—
reservations)

Customer Service Manager
Speed Queen Company
P.O. Box 990
Ripon, WI 54971-0990
414-748-3121
414-748-4053 (TDD)

Springs Industries Inc.
Springmaid/Performance
787 Seventh Avenue
New York, NY 10019
212-903-2100

Squibb; see Bristol-Myers Squibb
Pharmaceutical Group

Marketing Manager
Stanley Hardware
Division Stanley Works
480 Myrtle Street
New Britain, CT 06050
203-225-5111
800-622-4393 (toll free)

Manager, Consumer Information
    Center
Stouffer Foods Corporation
5750 Harper Road
Solon, OH 44139-1880
216-248-3600

Consumer Affairs
Sunbeam/Oster Household
    Products
P.O. Box 247
Laurel, MS 39441-0247
(written inquiries only)

Customer Service
Swatch Watch USA
1817 William Penn Way
Lancaster, PA 17604
717-394-5288

Supervisor, Consumer Affairs
3M
3M Center, Building 225-5N–04
St. Paul, MN 55144-1000
612-733-1871

Customer Service
Talbots
175 Beal Street

Hingham, MA 02043
800-992-9010 (toll free)
800-624-9179 (toll free TDD)

Director, Customer Relations
Tandy Corporation/Radio Shack
1400 One Tandy Center
Fort Worth, TX 76102
817-390-3218

Tappan Appliance Company, Inc.;
see The Frigidaire Co.

Consumer Relations and Quality
    Assurance
Target Stores
33 South Sixth Street
P.O. Box 1392
Minneapolis, MN 55440-1392
612-370-6056

Manager, Customer Relations
Texaco Refining and Marketing
P.O. Box 2000
Bellaire, TX 77401-2000
713-432-2235

Consumer Products
Texas Instruments Incorporated
P.O. Box 53
Lubbock, TX 79408-0053
806-741-3303
800-842-2737 (toll free)

Customer Service Representative
Thom McAn Shoe Co.
67 Millbrook Street

Worcester, MA 01606-2804
508-791-3811

Consumer Correspondent
Timex Corporation
P.O. Box 2740
Little Rock, AR 72203-2740
501-372-1111
800-367-9282 (toll free)

Supervisor, Consumer Affairs
Tonka Products
P.O. Box 200
Pawtucket, RI 02861-0200
800-248-6652 (toll free)

Director, Communications and
    Public Affairs
The Toro Company
8111 Lyndale Avenue South
Minneapolis, MN 55420
612-887-8900

Vice President of Service
Toshiba America Consumer
    Products, Inc.
Consumer Products Business Sector
1420 Toshiba Drive
Lebanon, TN 37087
615-449-2360

Consumer Affairs Manager
Totes, Incorporated
10078 East Kemper Road
Loveland, OH 45140
513-583-2300
800-282-2025

Corporate Spokesperson
Toys "R" Us
461 From Road
Paramus, NJ 07652
201-599-7897

Staff Vice President, Customer
    Relations
Trans World Airlines, Inc.
110 South Bedford Road
Mt. Kisco, NY 10549
914-242-3000
800-421-8480 (toll free TDD—
reservations)

Customer Services Department
Tupperware
P.O. Box 2353
Orlando, FL 32802
407-847-3111
800-858-7221 (toll free)

Manager, Consumer Relations
Tyson Foods
P.O. Box 2020
Springdale, AR 72765-2020
501-290-4714
800-233-6332 (toll free)

Vice President for Marketing
    Customer Service
U-Haul International
2727 North Central Avenue
Phoenix, AZ 85004-1120
800-528-0463

Manager, Consumer Affairs
Uniroyal Goodrich Tire Company

600 South Main Street
Akron, OH 44397-0001
216-374-3796
800-521-9796 (toll free)

Director of Customer Relations
United Airlines
P.O. Box 66100
Chicago, IL 60666
312-952-6168
800-323-0170 (toll free TDD—
reservations)

National Consumer Relations
    Manager
United Parcel Service of America,
    Incorporated
400 Perimeter Center
Terraces North
Atlanta, GA 30346
404-913-6000

Relocation Service
United Van Lines, Inc.
One United Drive
Fenton, MO 63026
800-325-3870 (toll free)

The Upjohn Company
Consumer Products Division (over-
    the-counter)
Patient Information (prescriptions)
7000 Portage Road
Kalamazoo, MI 49001
800-253-8600 (toll free)

Director, Consumer Affairs
USAir

P.O. Box 1501
Winston-Salem, NC 27102-1501
919-661-0061
703-892-7020

Supervisor, Executive Consumer
    Services
U.S. Sprint
8001 Stemmons Freeway
Dallas, TX 75247
214-688-5707
800-347-8988 (toll free)

Consumer Relations Department
Valvoline Oil Company
3499 Dabney Drive
P.O. Box 14000
Lexington, KY 40512
606-264-7777

Customer Relations
Visa USA, Inc.
P.O. Box 8999
San Francisco, CA 94128-8999
415-570-2900
(Cardholder should always call
issuing bank first.)

Consumer Affairs
Vons Companies Inc.
P.O. Box 3338
Los Angeles, CA 90051
818-821-7000

Manager Customer Relations
Walgreen Co.
200 Wilmot Road
Mail Stop 440

Deerfield, IL 60015
708-940-2927
800-289-2273 (toll free)

Customer Relations
Wal-Mart Stores, Inc.
702 S.W. Eighth Street
Bentonville, AR 72716-0117
501-273-4000

Director, Consumer Affairs
    Division
Warner-Lambert Company
201 Tabor Road
Morris Plains, NJ 07950
201-540-2459
800-223-0182 (toll free)
800-524-2624 (toll free — Parke
Davis products/over-the-counter)
800-742-8377 (toll free — Schick
    razor)
800-562-0266 (toll free — EPT)
800-223-0182 (toll free — Warner-
Lambert products)
800-524-2854 (toll free — Trident)
800-343-7805 (toll free TDD)

Consumer Relations Manager
Wendy's International, Inc.
P.O Box 256
Dublin, OH 43017-0256
614-764-6800

Manager of Consumer Information
West Bend Company
400 Washington Street
West Bend, WI 53095
414-334-2311

Director, Customer Relations
 Department
Whirlpool Corporation
2303 Pipestone Rd.
Benton Harbor, MI 49022-2427
616-926-5000
800-253-1301 (toll free)

White Westinghouse Appliances;
see The Frigidaire Co.

Customer Service
Williams-Sonoma
100 North Point Street
San Francisco, CA 94133
415-421-7900

Executive Vice President
Winn Dixie Stores Inc.
Box B
Jacksonville, FL 32203
904-783-5000

Customer Service
F.W. Woolworth Company
233 Broadway
New York, NY 10279-0001
212-553-2000

Consumer Affairs Administrator
Wm. Wrigley Jr. Company
410 North Michigan Avenue
Chicago, IL 60611
312-644-2121

Customer Relations
Xerox Corporation
100 Clinton Avenue South

Rochester, NY 14644
716-423-5480

Manager, Customer Relations
Yamaha Motor Corporation
6555 Katella Avenue
Cypress, CA 90630-5101
714-761-7439

Vice President, Consumer Affairs
Zenith Electronics Corporation
1000 Milwaukee Avenue
Glenview, IL 60025-2493
708-391-8100 (voice only)
800-488-8129 (toll free TDD only)

Car Complaints

You have two levels of protection here: your warranty and your state lemon law. The first will serve you well for the individual problem, but if the problems mount, you need to know your rights under your local lemon law. The following is a state-by-state summary of what you need to do before you can claim a refund or a brand-new vehicle.

Alabama

You qualify if you've had three unsuccessful repairs or your car has been out of service for thirty days within a twenty-four-month or 24,000-mile period, whichever is shorter. Send a certified letter invoking the lemon law to the automobile manufacturer, which then has fourteen days to make a final, effective, repair or replace the car. Call 800-392-5658 for more information.

Alaska

You qualify if you've had three unsuccessful repairs or your car has been out of service for more than thirty business days within one year or within sixty days of the expiration of your warranty, whichever is shorter. Send certified letters both to the automobile manufacturer and to your dealer within two months of the end of your warranty or within one year. Demand that you be given a full refund or a replacement vehicle within sixty days of the postmark on your letter. They are required to make a final repair attempt within thirty days of receiving your demand. Call 907-562-0704.

Arizona

You qualify if you've had three unsuccessful repairs or if your car has been out of service for thirty business days within a one-year period. Write to the automobile manufacturer invoking the lemon law to give them a chance to make a final repair. Call 602-542-5763.

Arkansas

You qualify if you've had three unsuccessful repairs or one unsuccessful repair of a defect that could cause death or serious injury within two years or 24,000 miles if the car is under warranty, whichever is shorter. Send a certified letter to the automobile manufacturer, which has ten days to notify you where to take the car for repair. That facility then has ten days to carry out a successful repair. Call 501-682-2341.

California

You qualify if you've had four unsuccessful repairs or your car has been out of service for thirty business days within a one-year/12,000-mile period, whichever is shorter. Send a certified letter to the automobile manufacturer and deliver your car to the repair facility they recommend within thirty days. Leased vehicles are included in this law. You have the option of submitting your complaint to arbitration. Call 916-322-3360.

Colorado

You qualify if you've had four unsuccessful repairs or your car has been out of service for thirty business days within one year or within your warranty period, whichever is shorter. You must be able to prove that you sent certified letters to the automobile manufacturer about each defect and that you offered them ample opportunity to complete the repairs. Call 303-866-5189.

Connecticut

You qualify if you've had four unsuccessful repairs, two unsuccessful repairs of a defect likely to cause death or serious injury within one year or the period of your warranty, whichever is shorter, or if your car has been out of service for thirty business days within a two-year/18,000-mile period, whichever is shorter. Notify the manufacturer or your dealer. Written notice to the manufacturer is required only if the warranty in your owner's manual so specifies. Call 203-566-7002.

Delaware

You qualify if you've had four unsuccessful repairs or your car has been out of service for thirty days within a one-year period or within your warranty, whichever is shorter. You must notify the automobile manufacturer and allow it the opportunity to repair your vehicle. Leased vehicles are covered. Call 302-577-3250.

District of Columbia

You qualify if you've had four unsuccessful repairs, one unsuccessful repair of a dangerous defect within two years or 18,000 miles, whichever is shorter, or your car has been out of service for thirty days within that same time period. You must report each problem to the manufacturer or dealer. Leased cars are included. You may choose arbitration. Contact: CAS Lemon Law, 2001 S Street, N. W., Washington, DC 20009.

Florida

You qualify if you've had three unsuccessful repairs or your car has been out of service for twenty days within one year/12,000 miles, whichever is shorter. You should send a certified or express mail letter to the automobile manufacturer, which has fourteen days (ten if the vehicle has been out of service for twenty days) after the delivery of your car to a designated dealer to attempt a final repair. Leased vehicles are included. You may choose arbitration. Call 800-321-5366.

Georgia

You qualify if you've had three unsuccessful repairs or your car has been out of service for thirty days within two years or 24,000 miles, whichever is shorter; if your car has been out of service for more than fifteen days within one year or 12,000 miles, whichever is shorter; or if you've had one unsuccessful repair of a serious safety defect in the brake or steering system within one year or 12,000 miles, whichever is shorter. Send a certified letter, return receipt requested, to the manufacturer, which has seven days to designate a repair facility. The repair facility has fourteen days to fix the car. Leased vehicles are included. You may choose arbitration. Call 404-656-3790.

Hawaii

You qualify if you've had three unsuccessful repairs, one unsuccessful repair of a defect likely to cause death or serious injury, or your car has been out of service for thirty days within two years or 24,000 miles, whichever is shorter. You must provide written notification to the automobile manufacturer and offer them the opportunity to repair the car. You may choose arbitration. Leased vehicles are included. Call 808-587-3222.

Idaho

You qualify if you've had four repair attempts or if your car has been out of service for thirty business days within one year or 12,000 miles, whichever is shorter. You must notify the manufacturer or dealer in writing. Call 208-334-2424.

Illinois

You qualify if you've had four repair attempts or if your car has been out of service for thirty business days within one year or 12,000 miles, whichever is shorter. You must notify the manufacturer in writing and offer them the opportunity to repair your vehicle. Call 217-782-9011.

Indiana

You qualify if you've had four unsuccessful repair attempts or if your car has been out of service for thirty business days within eighteen months or 18,000 miles, whichever is shorter. You must notify the manufacturer in writing only if your warranty requires that. Leased vehicles are included. Call 800-382-5516.

Iowa

You qualify if you've had three unsuccessful repair attempts, one unsuccessful repair of a defect likely to cause death or serious injury, or if your car has been out of service for twenty business days within two years or 24,000 miles, whichever is shorter. You must notify the manufacturer in writing and offer them an opportunity to repair the vehicle within ten days of their receipt of your letter. Leased vehicles are included. You may choose arbitration. Call 515-281-5926.

Kansas

You qualify if you've had four unsuccessful repair attempts of the same problem, ten repairs of any and all problems, or if your car has been out of service for thirty business days within one year or your warranty period, whichever is shorter. Send a notice to the manufacturer. Call 913-296-3751.

Kentucky

You qualify if you've had four unsuccessful repair attempts or if your car has been out of service for thirty business days within one year or 12,000 miles, whichever is shorter. Send a notice to the manufacturer. Call 502-573-2200.

Louisiana

You qualify if you've had four unsuccessful repair attempts or if your car has been out of service for thirty business days within one year or 12,000 miles, whichever is shorter. Send a notice to the manufacturer or dealer. Call 504-342-9638.

Maine

You qualify if you've had three unsuccessful repair attempts (if the same repair facility has worked on it at least twice) or if your car has been out of service for fifteen business days within two years or 18,000 miles, whichever is shorter. Send a notice to the manufacturer or dealer only if your warranty requires it. The manufacturer has seven business days after receipt of your letter to attempt final repair. Leased vehicles are included. You may choose arbitration. Call 207-626-8849.

Maryland

You qualify if you've had four unsuccessful repair attempts, one unsuccessful repair attempt of a serious safety defect in the braking or steering system, or if your car has been out of service for thirty business days within two years or 24,000 miles, whichever is shorter. Send a certified

letter, return receipt requested, to the manufacturer offering an opportunity to repair the vehicle within thirty days. Leased vehicles are included. Call 410-528-8662.

Massachusetts

You qualify if you've had three unsuccessful repair attempts or if your car has been out of service for fifteen business days within one year or 15,000 miles, whichever is shorter. Notify the dealer or manufacturer, which has seven business days to attempt a final repair. You may choose arbitration. Call 617-727-8400.

Michigan

You qualify if you've had four unsuccessful repair attempts or if your car has been out of service for thirty business days within one year or the period of your warranty, whichever is shorter. Send a certified letter, return receipt requested, to the manufacturer, which has five business days after receipt to repair the car. Call 517-373-1140.

Minnesota

You qualify if you've had four unsuccessful repairs, one unsuccessful repair of a major problem in the braking or steering system likely to cause death or serious injury, or your car has been out of service for thirty days within two years or the period of your warranty, whichever is shorter. Send at least one written notification to the manufacturer or dealer offering them the opportunity to repair your car. Leased vehicles are included. Call 612-296-3353.

Mississippi

You qualify if you've had three unsuccessful repairs or if your car has been out of service for fifteen business days within one year or the period of your warranty, whichever is shorter. Write to the manufacturer, which has ten business days to repair the car after its delivery to a designated dealer. Call 601-359-4230.

Missouri

You qualify if you've had four unsuccessful repairs or if your car has been out of service for thirty business days within one year or the period of your warranty, whichever is shorter. Write to the manufacturer, which has ten days to repair the car after its delivery to a designated dealer. Call 800-392-8222.

Montana

You qualify if you've had four unsuccessful repairs or if your car has been out of service for thirty business days within two years or 18,000 miles, whichever is shorter. Write to the manufacturer and offer an opportu-

nity for them to attempt a final repair. You can choose arbitration. Call 406-444-3553.

Nebraska

You qualify if you've had four unsuccessful repairs or if your car has been out of service for forty business days within a year or the period of your warranty, whichever is shorter. Send a certified letter to the manufacturer and offer an opportunity for them to attempt a final repair. Leased vehicles are included. Call 402-471-9593.

Nevada

You qualify if you've had four unsuccessful repairs or if your car has been out of service for thirty business days within a year or the period of your warranty, whichever is shorter. Send a letter to the manufacturer. Leased vehicles are included. Call 702-688-1800.

New Hampshire

You qualify if you've had three unsuccessful repairs by the same dealer or if your car has been out of service for thirty business days within the period of your warranty. Use the forms provided by the manufacturer to complain to the distributor and offer them a final repair opportunity. Leased vehicles are included. You may choose arbitration. Call 603-271-6383.

New Jersey

You qualify if you've had three unsuccessful repairs or your car has been out of service for twenty days within two years or 18,000 miles, whichever is shorter. Send a certified letter, return receipt requested, to the manufacturer, which has ten days to repair your car. Leased vehicles are included. You may choose arbitration. Call 201-504-6226.

New Mexico

You qualify if you've had four unsuccessful repairs or your car has been out of service for thirty days within one year or the period of your warranty, whichever is shorter. Notify the manufacturer or dealer in writing and offer them the opportunity to repair your vehicle. Call 505-827-6060.

New York

You qualify if you've had four unsuccessful repairs or your car has been out of service for thirty days within two years or 18,000 miles, whichever is shorter. Notify the manufacturer or dealer by certified letter. Leased vehicles are included. You may choose arbitration. Call 518-474-5481.

North Carolina

You qualify if you've had four unsuccessful repairs within two years or 24,000 miles, whichever is shorter, or if your car has been out of service for twenty business days during any twelve-month warranty period. Send a letter to the manufacturer and offer them the opportunity to repair the car within fifteen days of the receipt of your letter. Call 919-733-7741.

North Dakota

You qualify if you've had four unsuccessful repair attempts or if your car has been out of service for thirty business days after notification of the problem within one year or the period of the warranty, whichever is shorter. You must write to the manufacturer and offer them an opportunity to repair your car. Call 800-472-2600.

Ohio

You qualify if you've had three unsuccessful repair attempts of the same defect, a total of eight repairs of any type, one unsuccessful repair of a defect likely to cause death or serious injury, or if your car has been out of service for thirty business days within one year or 18,000 miles, whichever is shorter. Call 800-282-0515.

Oklahoma

You qualify if you've had four unsuccessful repair attempts or if your car has been out of service for forty-five days within one year or 12,000 miles, whichever is shorter. You must notify the manufacturer and offer them the opportunity to repair your car. Call 405-521-4274.

Oregon

You qualify if you've had four unsuccessful repair attempts or if your car has been out of service for thirty days within one year or within the warranty period, whichever is shorter. You must notify the manufacturer and offer them the opportunity to repair your car. Leased vehicles are included. Call 503-229-5576.

Pennsylvania

You qualify if you've had three unsuccessful repair attempts or if your car has been out of service for thirty days within one year or 12,000 miles, whichever is shorter. You must delivery your car to an authorized dealer. If you cannot, write the manufacturer or dealer, which must pay for delivery. Call 215-560-2414.

Rhode Island

You qualify if you've had four unsuccessful repair attempts or if your car has been out of service for thirty days within one year or 15,000 miles, whichever is shorter. You should complain to the manufacturer or dealer, which has seven days to attempt a final repair. Leased vehicles are included. Call 401-274-4400.

South Carolina

You qualify if you've had three unsuccessful repair attempts or if your car has been out of service for thirty days within one year or 12,000 miles,

whichever is shorter. Send a certified letter to the manufacturer and offer them the opportunity to repair the vehicle if informed that you are required to do so at the time of vehicle purchase. The manufacturer has ten days in which to refer you to a repair facility, which has ten more days to make a final repair. Leased vehicles are included. You may choose arbitration. Call 803-734-9452.

South Dakota

You qualify if you've had four unsuccessful repair attempts—at least one of which occurred within a one-year or a 12,000-mile period—or if your car has been out of service for thirty days within two years or 24,000 miles, whichever is shorter. Send a certified letter to the manufacturer and offer them the opportunity to repair the vehicle. The manufacturer has seven days in which to refer you to a repair facility, which has fourteen more days to make a final repair. If the manufacturer has a state-certified informal dispute-settlement procedure, you must use it before beginning legal action. Call 800-300-1986.

Tennessee

You qualify if you've had four unsuccessful repair attempts or your car has been out of service for thirty days within one year or the period of your warranty, whichever is shorter. Send a certified letter to the manufacturer

offering them ten days to attempt a
final repair. Leased vehicles are
included. Call 615-741-4737.

Texas

You qualify if you've had four unsuccessful repairs—two occurring within
the shorter time period of one year
or 12,000 miles and the other two
within the shorter time period of one
year or 12,000 miles from the date of
the second repair attempt—or two
unsuccessful repairs of a serious
safety defect with one occurring
within the shorter time period of one
year or 12,000 miles and the other
occurring within the shorter period
of one year or 12,000 miles from the
date of the first repair; or if your car
has been out of service for thirty days
within a period of two years or 24,000
miles, whichever is shorter, and at
least two repair attempts have been
made within one year or 12,000
miles, whichever is shorter. Notify
the manufacturer in writing. Leased
vehicles are included. You may
choose arbitration. Call 512-476-3618.

Utah

You qualify if you've had four unsuccessful repair attempts or your car
has been out of service for thirty business days within one year or the
period of your warranty, whichever is
shorter. Complain to the manufacturer or dealer. Leased vehicles are
included. Call 801-530-6601.

Vermont

You qualify if you've had three
unsuccessful repair attempts with at
least the first repair falling within the
warranty period, or if your car has
been out of service for thirty business
days within the period of your warranty. Forms are provided for you to
notify the manufacturer, which you
must do after the third attempted
repair or after you've reached thirty
days with the car out of service.
Arbitration must be held within
forty-five days after you've made
such notice. During that time the
manufacturer may make one final
repair attempt. Leased vehicles are
included. State-run arbitration is
available. Call 802-656-3183.

Virginia

You qualify if you've had three
unsuccessful repair attempts, one
repair attempt of a serious safety
defect, or your car has been out of
service for thirty days of an eighteen-
month period. Write to the manufacturer, which may make one final
repair attempt within thirty days.
Call 804-786-2042.

Washington

You qualify if you've had four unsuccessful repair attempts; two repairs of
serious safety defects first reported
within two years, 24,000 miles, or
your warranty period, whichever is
shorter; or your car has been out of

service for thirty days (fifteen days during your warranty period) during that same time period. One repair attempt and half of the thirty days must fall within the manufacturer's express warranty of at least one year or 12,000 miles. Write to the manufacturer and you should receive a replacement or refund within forty days. Leased vehicles are included. You can choose arbitration. Call 206-587-4240.

West Virginia

You qualify if you've had three unsuccessful repair attempts, one unsuccessful repair of a problem likely to cause death or serious injury, or your car has been out of service for thirty days within one year or the period of your warranty, whichever is shorter. You must write to the manufacturer and offer at least one opportunity to repair the vehicle. You may choose arbitration. Call 800-368-8808.

Wisconsin

You qualify if you've had four unsuccessful repairs or if your car has been out of service for thirty days within one year or the period of your warranty, whichever is shorter. Write to the manufacturer or dealer offering to return your title and you should receive a replacement or refund within thirty days. Leased vehicles are included. Call 608-266-0765.

Wyoming

You qualify if you've had three unsuccessful repair attempts or your car has been out of service for thirty business days within one year. Write to the manufacturer and offer them an opportunity to repair the vehicle. Call 307-777-7874.

Customer Relations Offices of Major Automobile Companies

ACURA
Customer Relations Department
1919 Torrance Boulevard
Torrance, CA 90501-2746
800-382-2238 (toll free)

Alfa-Romeo Distributors of North
America, Inc.
Customer Service Manager
8259 Exchange Drive
P.O. Box 598026
Orlando, FL 32859-8026
407-856-5000

American Honda Motor Company,
Inc.
Consumer Affairs Department
1919 Torrance Boulevard
Torrance, CA 90501-2746
213-783-3260

American Isuzu Motors, Inc.
Customer Relations Department
13181 Crossroads Parkway North

P.O. Box 2480
City of Industry, CA 91746-0480
310-699-0500
800-255-6727 (toll free)

American Motors Corporation; see
Jeep/Eagle Division of Chrysler
Motors Corporation

Attn: Customer Relations
    Department
American Suzuki Motor
    Corporation
3251 E. Imperial Highway
Brea, CA 92621-6722
Automobiles
800-934-0934 (toll free)
Motorcycles
714-996-7040, ext. 380

Audi of America, Inc.
Customer Relations—3E03
3800 Hamlin Road
Auburn Hills, MI 48326
General assistance and customer
relations
800-822-2834 (toll free)
Replacement and repurchase
assistance
800-955-5100 (toll free)

BMW of North America, Inc.
National Customer Relations
    Manager
P.O. Box 1227
Westwood, NJ 07675-1227
800-831-1117 (toll free)

Chrysler Motors Corporation
Ms. A. Tomlanovich
Chrysler Customer Center
Chrysler Corporation
P.O. Box 302
Center Line, MI 48015-9302
800-992-1997 (toll free)

Ferrari North America, Inc.
Mr. Kenneth McCay
Director of Service and Parts
250 Sylvan Avenue
Englewood Cliffs, NJ 07632
201-816-2650

Ford Motor Company
Customer Relations Manager
Ford Motor Company
300 Renaissance Center
P.O. Box 43360
Detroit, MI 48243
800-392-3673 (toll free—all
makes)
800-521-4140 (toll free—Lincoln
and Merkur only)
800-241-3673 (toll free—towing and
dealer location service)
800-232-5952 (toll free TDD)

Customer Assistance Center
Buick Motor Division
General Motors Corporation
902 East Hamilton Avenue
Flint, MI 48550
800-521-7300 (toll free)
800-TD-BUICK (toll free TDD)

202 Appendix B: Consumer Resources

Consumer Relations Center
Cadillac Motor Car Division
General Motors Corporation
30009 Van Dyke
P.O. Box 9025
Warren, MI 48090-9025
800-458-8006 (toll free)
800-TDD-CMCC (toll free TDD)

General Motors Corporation
Customer Assistance Center
Chevrolet/Geo Motor Division
General Motors Corporation
P.O. Box 7047
Troy, MI 48007-7047
800-222-1020 (toll free)
800-TDD-CHEV (toll free TDD)

Customer Service Department
GMC Truck Division
General Motors Corporation
Mail Code 1607-07
16 Judson Street
Pontiac, MI 48342
800-462-8782
800-GMC-TKTD (toll free TDD)

Customer Assistance Network
Oldsmobile Division
General Motors Corporation
P.O. Box 30095
Lansing, MI 48921
800-442-6537 (toll free)
800-TDD-OLDS (toll free TDD)

Customer Assistance Center
Pontiac Division
General Motors Corporation

One Pontiac Plaza
Pontiac, MI 48340-2952
800-762-2737 (toll free)
800-TDD-PONT (toll free TDD)

Saturn Assistance Center
Saturn Corporation
General Motors Corporation
100 Saturn Parkway
Spring Hill, TN 37174
800-553-6000 (toll free)
800-TDD-6000 (toll free TDD)

Honda; see American Honda
Motor Company, Inc.

Hyundai Motor America
Customer Service
10550 Talbert Avenue
P.O. Box 20850
Fountain Valley, CA 92728-0850
800-633-5151 (toll free)

Isuzu; see American Isuzu Motors,
Inc.

Jaguar Cars Inc.
555 MacArthur Boulevard
Mahwah, NJ 07430-2327
201-818-8500

Jeep/Eagle Division of Chrysler
Motors Corporation; see Chrysler
Motors Corporation

Mazda Motor of America, Inc.
Corporate Headquarters: Customer
    Relations Manager

P.O. Box 19734
Irvine, CA 92718
800-222-5500 (toll free)

Mercedes Benz of North America,
    Inc.
Customer Assistance Center
1 Glenview Road
Montvale, NJ 07645
201-476-6200

Mitsubishi Motor Sales of America,
    Inc.
National Consumer Relations
    Manager
6400 West Katella Avenue
Cypress, CA 90630-5208
800-222-0037 (toll free)

Nissan Motor Corporation in USA
P.o. Box 191
Gardena, CA 90248-0191
800-647-7261 (toll free—all
consumer inquiries)

Peugeot Motors of America, Inc.
Mr. William J. Atanasio
National Customer Relations
    Manager
P.O. Box 607
One Peugeot Plaza
Lyndhurst, NJ 07071-3498
201-935-8400
800-345-5549 (toll free)

Porsche Cars North America, Inc.
Manager, Owner Relations

100 West Liberty Street
P.O. Box 30911
Reno, NV 89520-3911
800-545-8039

Saab Cars USA, Inc.
Customer Assistance Center
4405-A Saab Drive
P.O. Box 9000
Norcross, GA 30091
800-955-9007 (toll free)

Subaru of America, Inc.
National Customer Service Center
Subaru Plaza
P.O. Box 6000
Cherry Hill, NJ 08034-6000
800-SUBARU3 (toll free)
800-782-2783 (toll free)

Suzuki; see American Suzuki
Motor Corporation

Toyota Motor Sales, Inc.
Customer Assistance Center
Toyota Motor Sales USA, Inc.
Department A102
19001 South Western Avenue
Torrance, CA 90509
800-331-4331 (toll free)

Volkswagen United States, Inc.
Customer Relations—2F02
3800 Hamlin Road
Auburn Hills, MI 48326
General assistance and customer
relations
800-822-8987 (toll free)

Replacement and repurchase assistance
800-955-5100 (toll free)

Volvo Cars of North America
Corporate Office: Consumer
    Affairs
P.O. Box 914
Rockleigh, NJ 07647-0914
201-767-4737
800-458-1552

Trade Associations

Sometimes, if you need to put a little bit of extra pressure on a company, you'll find it in an inquiry from a trade association. It is hardly foolproof, since these groups are often cheering squads for industry, but it is worth a try.

American Health Care Association
1201 L Street, N.W.
Washington, DC 20005-4014
202-842-4444
800-321-0343 (toll free—
publications only)

American Hotel and Motel
    Association
1201 New York Avenue, N.W.
Suite 600
Washington, DC 20005-3931
(written inquiries only)

Mr. Herbert A. Finkston, Director
Professional Ethics Division

American Institute of Certified
    Public Accountants
Harborside Financial Center
201 Plaza III
Jersey City, NJ 07311-3881
201-938-3175

Automotive Consumer Action
Program (AUTOCAP)
8400 Westpark Drive
McLean, VA 22102
703-821-7144

Consumer Affairs
Blue Cross and Blue Shield
    Association
1310 G Street, N.W., 12th Floor
Washington, DC 20005
202-626-4780

Ms. Caroline C. Ajootian
Director, Consumer Protection
    Bureau
Boat Owners Association of the
    United States
Boat/U.S.
880 South Pickett Street
Alexandria, VA 22304-0730
703-823-9550

Mr. Robert M. Fells, Assistant
    Secretary
Cemetery Consumer Service
    Council
P.O. Box 3574
Washington, DC 20007
703-379-6426

Ms. Marsha Goldberger, Director
Ethics and Consumer Affairs
Direct Marketing Association
  (DMA)
1101 Seventeenth Street, N.W.
Suite 705
Washington, DC 20037
(written complaints only)

Major Appliance Consumer Action
  Panel (MACAP)
20 North Wacker Drive
Chicago, IL 60606
312-984-5858
800-621-0477 (toll free)

Ms. Katherine L.J. Hoffman
Associate Director of Consumer
  Affairs
National Association of Professional
  Insurance Agents
400 North Washington Street
Alexandria, VA 22314

National Tire Dealers and
  Retreaders Association
1250 Eye Street, N.W.
Suite 400
Washington, DC 20005
202-789-2300
800-876-8372 (toll free)

Department of Consumer Affairs
National Turkey Federation
11319 Sunset Hills Road
Reston, VA 22090-5227
(written inquiries only)

Mrs. Jane Meyer
Director of Consumer Affairs
The Soap and Detergent Association
475 Park Avenue South
New York, NY 10016
212-725-1262

Tele-Consumer Hot Line
1910 K Street, N.W., Suite 610
Washington, D.C. 20006
202-223-4371 (voice/TDD)

Ms. Marisa Cascio
Communications Associate
Toy Manufacturers of America
200 Fifth Avenue, Room 740
New York, NY 10010
212-675-1141

Mr. Robert E. Whitley, President
U.S. Tour Operators Association
  (USTOA)
211 East 51st Street, Suite 12-B
New York, NY 10022
212-944-5727

About the Authors

FRANK BRUNI and ELINOR BURKETT first joined forces to terrorize American businesses while students at the Graduate School of Journalism at Columbia University. Bruni has since sowed the seeds of revolution in Detroit, where he worked as a reporter for the *Detroit Free Press*, and in New York City, where he currently writes for the *New York Times*. Burkett, meanwhile, fomented rebellion in South Florida as a reporter for the *Miami Herald*. She now lives in the Catskill Mountains, where the building of her dream home forced her to hone her skills as one of the nation's leading consumer terrorists. In her free time, she wrote *The Gravest Show on Earth: America in the Age of AIDS*, and is currently completing *ReRighting Feminism: A Political Travelogue Through Conservative America*. Bruni and Burkett's previous collaboration was a work of investigative journalism, *A Gospel of Shame: Children, Sexual Abuse and the Catholic Church*.